Responsio Iudaeorum Nostrae Aetatis
Response from The Jewish People of Our Time
Eternally Accused
of Conspiring to Kill Jesus

The Case Against the Gospels' False Accusation
A NEW DEFENSE BASED ON RECENT SCHOLARSHIP
IN THE MATTER OF HIS ARREST, JUDGMENT AND CRUCIFIXION

Responsio Iudaeorum Nostrae Aetatis
Response from The Jewish People of Our Time
Eternally Accused
of Conspiring to Kill Jesus

The Case Against the Gospels' False Accusation
A NEW DEFENSE BASED ON RECENT SCHOLARSHIP
IN THE MATTER OF HIS ARREST, JUDGMENT AND CRUCIFIXION

Abram Epstein

Responsio Iudaeorum Nostrae Aetatis
Response from The Jewish People of Our Time
Eternally Accused
of Conspiring to Kill Jesus

The Case Against the Gospels' False Accusation
A NEW DEFENSE BASED ON RECENT SCHOLARSHIP
IN THE MATTER OF HIS ARREST, JUDGMENT AND CRUCIFIXION

iUniverse books may be ordered through booksellers or by contacting:

iUniverse
1663 Liberty Drive
Bloomington, IN 47403
www.iuniverse.com
844-349-9409

Because of the dynamic nature of the Internet, any web addresses or links contained in
this book may have changed since publication and may no longer be valid. The views
expressed in this work are solely those of the author and do not necessarily reflect the
views of the publisher, and the publisher hereby disclaims any responsibility for them.

Any people depicted in stock imagery provided by Getty Images are models,
and such images are being used for illustrative purposes only.
Certain stock imagery © Getty Images.

Cover design: Abram Epstein

ISBN: 978-1-5320-9742-3 (sc)
ISBN: 978-1-5320-9743-0 (e)

Library of Congress Control Number: 2020921127

Print information available on the last page.

iUniverse rev. date: 08/12/2020

In Memoriam of Jesus who died teaching Hebrew heritage even as the spiritual Star of David was forced from his hands to form a crucifix, its every timber hewn from false accusation, until Jewish complicity became canonized as murder by his own People.

CONTENTS

FOREWORD

Prior to this treatise, and quite possibly forever after, the quiet contempt hovering over all natural goodwill between traditional Christians and Jews shall have arisen from one primary source: A theological, canonized "testament," the Gospels, or "good news," apprising the world God's Kingdom has been ushered in by the appearance of his Son who is said to have died for the sins of humanity and served as a model for the faithful to achieve salvation. A sanctified, graphic rendering of bloodthirsty Jews seeking, clamoring for and orchestrating his arrest and crucifixion permeate the passages read throughout the liturgical year in most churches. Few decent, traditional Christians have reason to doubt the Jews played a significant role in attempting to murder their Son of God.

To estimate the dimension of so centrally situated a sanctified doctrine as that accumulation of hateful passages implicating the Jews in Jesus' murder, one need only revisit the text of the "Nostra Aetate" (literally: "in our time") issued by Vatican II in 1965. After several years of struggling with its conscience over the hate which the Gospels have produced, leading to the Inquisition, the Crusades (not only against Moslems), ghetto-ization, and ultimately the Holocaust the final edict could only agree Jesus would forgive the Jews upon his Second Coming–and therefore in anticipation of his doing so, all good Christians should show faith the Jews are no longer to be despised for "pressing for the death of Christ." Subsequent "ameliorative" comments by church leaders focusing blame on only "those Jews contemporaneous to Jesus and not the entire modern-day Jewish People" fail to relieve the onus historically resonant in the Gospels' alleged declaration of infamy by the Jewish nation for all time, "His blood be on us and on our children/descendants" recorded in Matthew 27:25.

The Vatican II conclusion did far more to preserve the Gospels' venom towards the Jews than it did to reassess the canonized verdict of their having sought and orchestrated Jesus' state-sanctioned murder, confirming, "...All should see to it that, in catechetical work and in the preaching of the word of God, they teach nothing save what conforms to the truth of the gospel and the spirit of Christ."

Left to this treatise, therefore, was this author's responsibility to finally answer three centuries-old questions which have been inaccessible beneath Gospel layers of textual alteration and fragmentation: Who killed Jesus and why? And, what role, if any, did Jews play? With no ill-will guiding my work, only scrupulous objectivity, I urge all open-minded people to consider seriously what follows.

Responsio Iudaeorum Nostrae Aetatis is the first analytical document deconstructing and fully refuting the Gospel passages alluding to Jewish intent and actual participation in subduing, trying and executing Jesus.

Formatted as a legal brief, the treatise opens with a statement of purpose.

Accordingly, the following claim is unequivocal: textual proof shall be substantiated that there was no complicity in the arrest, hearing, judgment or crucifixion of Jesus by any Jews motivated by their Jewish origins to prevent the revelation he was God's anointed

King. Nor did any Jews conspire to achieve his demise based on a theological incentive to silence his teaching or terminate his ministerial activity.

Concerning the method of investigation

[Currently, the standard technique used to distinguish historical veracity from altered textual enhancement in Gospel descriptions still depends on the "Documentary Method" (considered by this author, ill-suited to meet the requirements of uncovering facts concealed beneath the Gospels' exposition). That method employs inference based on comparison between the variant texts drawn upon to support the theologian/scholar's hypothesis about Jesus' life and death. A confining parameter is the method's insufficient condition for achieving conclusions with any corroboration other than the accumulated "data"–namely, those passages taken at face value which form the basis of untestable hypothetical notions, put forth as "educated" supposition, often guided by a religious agenda, or intuition. Augmenting the weakness of such untestable hypotheses, the interpreters bring endless cultural parallels from the surrounding milieu, whether drawn from pre-Roman religious contexts, from the Hebrew Bible, or early church doctrines, Gnostic writings, anti-heretical polemics, apocryphal Jewish literature or other contemporaneous sources. But, the foundation of their edifice, as Jesus would have said, is built on sand. This author submits that no theorist can logically vote 'thumbs up or down' on the truth. The truth is either true, or it isn't.]

Responsio Iudaeorum, quite in distinction to other inquiries, relies on an altogether significant advance in critical Gospel analysis to achieve a level of certainty about what actually happened to Jesus, and who was responsible. For the first time a proposed description of an episode, its sequential context, historical embellishments, or, its complete lack of veracity have become largely testable.

The method, described in this author's book, "A Documented Biography of Jesus Before Christianity," is labeled, "Precipitous Insight." It is based on a logical assessment of considered passages each of which may contain a serious element of obscurity, seemingly shrouded in the mist of antiquity, which when taken as having been severed from the context of meaning shared by similarly "opaque" passages, when reassembled become contextually luminous. Their clarity, as one passage precipitates obvious, sudden meaning in both, is taken as an indication of likely historic authenticity. For a comparison, one may think of a court case with compounding circumstantial items of evidence, by themselves of doubtful significance, which taken together, lead toward an inescapable and clear conclusion.

Here is an example from the treatise:

As with any murder investigation–and the investigation of Jesus' death is nothing less–a primary focus must be on identifying any possible witness to the crime, and uncovering the motives which may have led the perpetrator to commit the deed itself.

To that end, Gospel texts containing obscure, descriptive elements obliquely referencing a "witness" have been thematically reassembled in **Responsio Iudaeorum.**

Among the fragments of central interest are those which reference witnesses to the travail Jesus suffered during his final day, with especial attention paid to the interrogation by Caiaphas. Based on the Gospel portrayal of Jews expressing deep contempt during the proceeding, one may justifiably raise the question: Who was inside the High Priest's house to make record and transcribe what occurred which became the Gospel account?

Indeed, even a cursory reading of the scene (described in all four canonical Gospels), indicates Simon/Peter never entered the house where the hearing was conducted. And, all four Gospels provide the whereabouts of Simon/Peter during the interrogation. He was in the exterior courtyard with the guards, according to Luke 22:55 and John 18:18, warming himself by the fire.

Only the Gospel of John reveals who the witness was. John 18:15 reads:

> "Simon/Peter and another *Disciple* (my italics) followed Jesus (to the house of Caiaphas). Since that Disciple was known to the High Priest, he went with Jesus into the courtyard...but Peter was standing outside the gate. So the other Disciple who was known to the High Priest went out (from the house) spoke to the woman who guarded the gate and brought Peter in to the courtyard (where he could warm himself by the fire). (18:18)

Who, then, was the witness in the house?

Until we search the last passage of the Gospel of John in an altogether fragmented context, the name of the "Disciple-witness" remains beyond grasp. Reassembled for thematic coherency, John 18:15 (above), achieves historical value.

21:20 reads:

> "Peter turned and saw the Disciple who Jesus loved...
> (and continuing, said):

"This is the Disciple who is testifying to these things
and has written them and we know that his testimony
is true."

Because the above passage describes the "Disciple who Jesus
loved" as a witness and scribe for the group, and actually names him
"the Disciple," the same as the one so-named entering Caiaphas'
house (the only Disciple who was inside as a witness) the combined
fragments now reach the level of hypothesis. If there was an individual
who had the authority to enter the house of Caiaphas and intercede in
behalf of Simon/Peter that he might warm himself by the courtyard
fire, that individual, identified in John (21:20) as a witness recording
testimony, would be the one our investigation had been seeking to
identify.

The conclusive, "precipitous" text occurs in I Acts 1:20-21:

Simon/Peter ceremoniously chose Matthias to be the *episkopas* or
supervisor of the Disciples' affairs, inviting him to be the twelfth as
a replacement for Judas Iscariot. The implication of the words when
combined with the above passages are profound:

"Let another take (Judas) place (to be) overseer (or,
'administrator') so one who has accompanied us
during all the time that the Lord Jesus went in and
out among us beginning from the Baptism of John
until the day he was taken up will become a witness
(to the resurrection)..."

Based on Matthias receiving the designation "officiating
administrator" (*episkopas*), one is aware he likely seemed to
Simon/Peter a sensible twelfth Disciple, with scribal skills and

commensurate Temple connections which earlier would enable him to enter Caiaphas' house and witness the hearing.

The three texts may now be joined to achieve "precipitous insight":

1. "The Disciple" who enters Caiaphas' house for the hearing has authority and is a witness (John 18:15).
2. "The Disciple Jesus loved" is a witness and scribe (and therefore has Temple connections; John 21:20; 21:24). He is identified in the passage as "the Disciple" (the same as the witness who had authority to enter the hearing in the High Priest's house).
3. Matthias is an administrator who, according to Simon/Peter has been with Jesus the whole time (I Acts 1:20-21). He is described by the term: "witness" suggesting his role will be to provide testimony.

Noteworthy is the fact that Matthias had his name totally expunged from the Gospels, leaving "the Disciple" and "the Disciple Jesus loved" as a reliquary of mysterious eponyms.

One assumes whatever breach of good will led to canonizing Matthias' anonymity was serious. That his name was preserved in one instance only, to make record of his filling Judas' vacancy, attests, more than likely, to several of their group demanding his recognition, owing to Jesus' love for him.

[Let the reader not mistake the first-ever identification of the name "Matthias" with the long-concealed "Disciple Jesus loved" for being a central purpose of this corpus. His emerging in the course of the investigation with a persona Gospel sleuths have sought to discover, here bears only on his role as a primary witness and record-keeper in solving the crime of Jesus' state-sanctioned murder on the cross and absolving the Jews of any participation in the crime.]

Among the many remarkable fragments the treatise reassembles for the first time are those illuminating the causal chain of events leading to Jesus' arrest.

As surprising as it may be to the church fathers who for millennia have immersed themselves in the sacred liturgical belief the Pharisees, consorting with elders, along with a God-forsaken "Council" (presumably the Sanhedrin), and Temple Priests were pressing to kill their Christ, the perpetrator who with premeditated guile and motivation actually plotted to have Jesus killed in a state-sanctioned murder– was no Hebrew at all.

The "voice" of Matthias, heard in disparate textual fragments, has enabled the investigation of **Responsio Iudaeorum** to track Jesus' fateful turn of events which commenced just following the winter of John the Baptist's arrest, during the early spring (most probably), 32 C.E.

Following heretofore opaque descriptions, a sequence emerges leading step-by-step, to the first-ever evidence which implicates his actual murderer.

Unlike John, whose political harangues according to Josephus, were the basis for a capital charge, and whose incarceration ended with his beheading, Jesus had never put himself in mortal danger by committing an act of sedition. Although the Gospels emphasize Jesus' recondite identity as "King of the Jews" (the "anointed one") was to be secret until the chosen hour, lest he suffer an "untimely" death outside Jerusalem, one of his own Disciples would spread a rumor about him which ultimately cost his life.

Although Christian theology offers no evidence to explain why Jesus was arrested, his alleged claim to be "King of the Jews" pronounced by Caiaphas, the High Priest, and then, by Pontius Pilate appear to be a charge of sedition based on villainous accusations brought by Jews determined to see him crucified.

In fact there were no such accusations, and the charge, as put forth in the Gospel rendering, rises out of "thin air."

Without providing details of the investigation in this Forward, as the case is fully elaborated in the body of the work, one should not let pass the remarkable revelation that according to Matthias' substantiated testimony, Jews not only did not participate in or seek Jesus' death, but tried to save him. From his textual account, one may observe, Jewish witnesses who wished to see Jesus die needed only testify he claimed to be "King of the Jews." Matthias records: They all refused to do so.

Further, the High Priest's vindictive and callous act of holding the hearing and turning Jesus over to Pilate for the pre-arranged verdict, is shown to have a non-Jewish motive, and was contrary to the wishes of the Jews present, who did not wish to be complicit in his criminality by bearing false witness.

Almost seamlessly that tapestry of Gospel horrors which commenced with Jesus' arrest in the Garden of Gethsemane, spread from the hearing to the judgment before Pontius Pilate and ultimately reached Golgotha.

Without evidence supporting an actual motive for wanting to kill Jesus, the lurid passages conjure such fabricated Jewish motives as "envy," or a burning contempt that "he equated himself with God," or, venomous priests, scribes, Temple leaders and crowds seeking his death to prove he was not the Son of God.

Again, turning to the fragmented text, a repository of actual recollections observed directly and left as scattered testimony throughout the Gospels, this treatise uncovers the seminal origin of blame for Jesus' crucifixion. What has now been proved beyond refutable conclusion, and laid before you, the jury, is the true account of the perpetrator, his motive and historical circumstances leading to Jesus' execution.

Bearing in mind the textual analysis of **Responsio Iudaeorum** purports to have achieved a temporal penetration of the Gospels' historical timeframe occurring during Jesus' ministry and terminating with the immediate aftermath of his crucifixion, I am obliged to contrast this treatise's significant advance in critical interpretation with the parameters of what has preceded it.

Succinctly, the panoply of general scholarship has considered the earliest entries in the Gospels to be based on "Jesus-as-the-Christ" kerygmata arising in the early 30's CE, several years postmortem. **Responsio Iudaeorum** has, contrary to this formerly a-priori supposition, unearthed a complex, fragmented, but syntactically coherent description of the contemporaneous events endangering Jesus and ultimately leading to his crucifixion. Further, the consequent illumination of these remarkable and historic underpinnings of the notorious murder-on-the-cross, exposes the true perpetrator, as well as revealing the first advent of christological justification of Jesus as having died with Jewish complicity. Central to the treatise before you, that supposed conspiratorial role by the Jews is fully exposed through meticulous, critical deconstruction of the passages containing the relevant defamatory portrayals.

Simon/Peter understood the implications of the Jewish rejection of Jesus as God's Son.

Because their widespread influence could threaten to kill faith in him as the Christ, the fledgling theology appeared to be in desperate need of doctrinal rebuke of the Jewish relationship to God.

To prevent the looming calamity, Simon/Peter collaborated with those who attempted to save the Son of God from pervasive Jewish "rejection." Jews as "killers of faith" in his Divinity, metamorphosed into actual, bloodthirsty ghouls plotting and clamoring for Jesus' crucifixion.

The textual gore was a literary tactic intended to threaten prospective proselytes with the hovering talons of the Jewish satan, waiting to pounce and carry them off. The Gospel authors/editors under Simon/Peter's supervision, leading a Jerusalem "movement" small and foundering, with perhaps no more than five hundred followers, would do whatever was necessary to save Jesus as the Christ from the malign disinterest of the vast majority of Jews who simply were not joining the new religion.

One must ask, when considering the consensual scholars' assertion that the Disciples and certain apostles began their theological musings–to presumably become a later collection of recollections known as the 'Gospels'– at least three years after the crucifixion (measured from the apparent first manifestation of a "Jerusalem movement"), what were they doing during the time they were struck down with grief by the death of their messiah on the cross?

In substance, varied scholars share a view that as the fissures of difference widened between Jerusalem (personified by Peter) and Paul (considered to be in favor of dispensing utterly with Torah) one essential issue faced the postmortem group of Jesus' devotees three years and more after his death on the cross: whether to abide by Jewish law (such as dietary provisions and circumcision) or not, in order to be included as members of the fledgling church.

With the deepest respect for the many worthy studies and their conclusions, not intending to either dispute or advocate for any disparate views among them, one can hardly conjure it taking three years following the state-sanctioned murder-on-the-cross for Jesus' devotees, those who knew and loved him, to begin sitting together to meditate on his life and teachings and recollect what he had said and done. The scribal transcription of their varied accounts, according to **Responsio Iudaeorum,** recorded at the outset, were not blank as has been formerly believed. Much of what occurred has been reassembled in the treatise you are about to read.

A final word must be addressed to the reaction Jews had to the emergence of the Jesus-as-Christ movement in Jerusalem, at its outset, when Simon/Peter's antagonistic attitude led to the textual Gospel defamation. Although there were Jews who did eventually form small movements (eg. The Ebionites, others) in worshipping Jesus as the Christ, and much has been made of those who both considered him to have been resurrected and those who thought he was an "apocalyptic prophet," almost all Jews were simply not swayed toward the new faith. No archeological evidence exists that there were churches in the earliest period in the region where Jesus had lived, the Galilee. The negative influence of traditional Jews on Simon/Peter's prospective proselytes was a significant threat. Their rejection of Jesus as ever claiming to have been "King of the Jews" had, as the treatise expounds, earned them the stigma "killers of faith" in Jesus as the Christ, which, as expounded in the treatise, became a sanctified, canonized warning to would-be members of the fledgling church not to emulate the Jews who were "killers of faith-in- Jesus" ipso facto "Killers of Jesus."

READER'S GUIDE

The purpose: to present the case for complete acquittal of Jews portrayed in the Gospels as seeking the death of Jesus.

As the treatise states:

> *Jewish denial of Jesus' divine origin, portrayed in the four canonized Gospels of the New Testament, Matthew, Mark, Luke and John, has awakened in vast numbers of presumably decent, church-going Christians, a faith–indoctrinated certainty our unwitting purpose on earth was to sacrifice the lamb of God, and in causing Jesus' death, accomplish his Divine Plan to take away the sins of mankind, so that even us Jews today, still tainted, shall only be forgiven on the day we bear witness to the truth of his identity as God's only Son.*

As depicted in the Gospels, the Jew has been liturgically demonized in sanctified church services and sermons, quoting the sacred canon as "pressing for the death of Christ," spawning hatred in countless Christian hearts and minds, stimulating vast hordes to carry out crusades of annihilation against the Jewish People as the satanic "anti-Christ," building walls of imprisoning ghettoization, conducting inquisitions, forcing conversion or death, deporting entire populations into exile, slaughtering the innocent in pogrom massacres and ultimately exterminating millions in the gas chambers of the Holocaust.

Based on recent scholarship, the "DEFENSE" mounted in this treatise is the first to recover actual textual evidence resolving the following historic issues:

1. Who orchestrated the arrest, hearing and judgment of Jesus?
2. What was the perpetrator's motive?
3. What role did the Jews play?
4. Why were the Jews portrayed as bloodthirsty villains determined to see Jesus die?

The sections which comprise the corpus of the treatise.

Part One: A brief survey of the contemporary Catholic guidance concerning the Jewish role in Jesus' travail as expressed in the Vatican II formulary, "Nostra Aetatis."

In sum, the 1965 Vatican formulation Jews should be forgiven "in our time" pending their salvation upon Jesus' Second Coming (a matter of Catholic doctrine) amounts to reaffirming the accusation the Jews sought and abetted his death on the cross.

The conceptual Gospel doctrine more recently elaborated by the Church, and borrowing inspiration from the writings of Paul, perceive the ultimate fate of Judaism is to be subsumed and superseded by the Covenant with Jesus as the Christ. This vision of Christian supremacy justifies a never-ending faith in the veracity of the Gospel portrayal of Jews, whose spiritual vacuity and inherently malign natures made them servants of satan. Instead of seeking the evidentiary path illuminated in this work, the Church has sanctified the Gospels' most heinous view.

The Vatican's claim to an ecumenical achievement, "Nostra Aetate," expresses the hope and belief Jews shall share the epiphany to occur upon Jesus' descent from Heaven as the "Son of Man" when we may overcome the relics of our forlorn past, confinement by Torah and rabbinic laws, and accept communion with the body of Christ, rapturously redeemed by "Grace" as righteous and eternal in God's Kingdom.

Part Two: Blaming the Jews for the arrest, judgment and crucifixion of Jesus.

The canonical Gospel passages which have become the basis for accusing the Jews of "pressing for the death of Christ" (in the words of the Vatican's 1965 edict) are recapitulated and duly presented as exhibits of the canonical/Church doctrine of contempt toward the Jews.

A. Early in his ministry, narrative texts (selectively) include:

(They/the Jews) "...conspired how to destroy him..."
"were seeking to kill him..."
"were out to kill him..."

The egregious transgression supposedly arousing Jewish ire toward Jesus, was his supposed violation of the Torah commandment not to work on the Shabbat, which, according to the rabbis, included his performance of healings (Eg. Mark 3:6). Not only did he heal diseases on the Shabbat, and appear to make himself an authority over the Torah law but he cured afflictions of "punishment" such as blindness (John 5:1) by forgiving sin (accomplished, as the narrative text indicates, claiming authority from God as his "father.")

B. Sources of textual hate commencing with the sequence at the outset of Jesus' final journey to Jerusalem:

Jesus is quoted as telling the Disciples: (Mark 8:31-32 //'s) "(He must go to Jerusalem) and undergo great suffering, and be rejected/ at the hands of the elders, chief priests and scribes, and be killed...."

The Hearing and Interrogation of Jesus in the High Priest's House:

Caiaphas, the High Priest, who conducted the hearing in his house, supposedly pre-arranges the outcome with Pharisees and (chief) priests, meeting with the "council," saying, "It is better for you that one man should die on behalf of the people than the whole nation..."

Inside, according to the Gospel record (Matthew 26:59 and Mark 14:55):

> "The chief priests and whole council were looking for false testimony against Jesus so that they might put him to death. But they found none.

Matthew continuing:

> "Though many false witnesses came forward."

Mark continuing:

> "For many gave false testimony against him and their testimony did not agree."

To those Gospel editors accusing the Jews of wanting to see Jesus' crucified, their "false testimony" (the Gospel description) evokes their rabid anger as they attempt to make up something upon which to base the charge of sedition, causing him to be found guilty and executed. Even if they did not have any evidence against him, the Gospels would have us believe, the venomous Jews at that hearing would turn Jesus' innocence to guilt. From an altogether different perspective, however, one recognizes that they were refusing to bear false witness. After all, if they wished to see Jesus die, all they had to do was say, "He claimed to be 'King of the Jews.'"

[IMPORTANT NOTE: Despite there having been no witnesses testifying they ever heard Jesus claim to be "King of the Jews" (the crime of sedition for which he was charged) he was led off to be judged and sentenced by Pontius Pilate. The failure by Caiaphas to establish such testimony appears to have caused him deep consternation and is reflected in the narrative of the Gospel of Mark 14:63: "Then the High Priest tore his clothes and said, 'Why do we still need witnesses?'"]

Still, as if his non-confessional reply suffices, Caiaphas is said to inquire of the gathered Jews, "What is your verdict?"

"They answered, 'He deserves death.'" (Matthew 26:65-66)

C. The narrative dramatizing hateful (chief) priests, the "council," scribes, Pharisees, elders and crowds clamoring for the death of Jesus:

Although there is a paucity of witnesses testifying Jesus committed the crime of sedition, while Mark 14:55 indicates "the whole council" was present, and (telling from Caiaphas' frustration) might have done so at the hearing. Even when Jesus is brought before Pontius Pilate and the "council" supposedly chooses to speak up, they still do not accuse him of claiming to be "King of the Jews. They say only (Luke 23:5): "He stirs up the people, teaching throughout all Judea, from Galilee where he began, even to this place."

During the interrogation, both inside Caiaphas house, and then before Pontius Pilate, Jesus replies to the question: "Do you say you are 'King of the Jews,' with the words, 'You have said so,' or, 'They are your words.' (One exception, when he says 'I am' is regarded as an extrapolation from a more lengthy reply taken out of context and deconstructed in the treatise.)

Jesus is interrogated by Pilate and after being mocked by a cohort of soldiers, Jews explain to Pilate he deserves to be crucified because he has broken a law by "claiming to be the Son of God." (John 19:7)

Pontius Pilate's attempt to crucify a murderous infidel named Barabbas instead of Jesus, as a gesture of good will on Passover, does not placate the bloodthirsty Jews who refuse to accept any substitute for God's Son.

Finally, Pilate reluctantly gives in to the ghoulish crowd, including priests and scribes, shouting, "Crucify him. Crucify him" (John 19:6).

On the high hill of crucifixion known as Golgotha, the grim scene of his slowly expiring is accompanied by scribes and elders (Matthew 27:41) chief priests (Mark 15:31-32) and Jewish leaders (Luke 23:35) taking solace from the misery he suffers, portrayed as a visual cause for taunting and making jokes at his supposed claim to be "King of the Jews," the charge for which he is crucified, stated on the cross along with his residential origin as a Nazarene.

Part three: Identifying the perpetrator of Jesus' grim demise.

The critical analysis used to recover the identity and role of a primary witness constitutes an opening segment of the case exposing the actual murderer and acquitting the Jews of all participation. (Note: Caiaphas' role in handing over Jesus to Pilate for judgment shall be shown to have had no theological motive, nor one provoked by Jewish popular sentiment.)

The Caiaphas' interrogation-record of far-less than capital accusations which appear (in any event) to be likely fabrications, such as, "We heard him say he would destroy this Temple..." (Mark 14:58) indicate an objective witness was detailing the absence of any testimony necessary for Jesus' execution. By applying strict standards of textual analysis to that set of circumstances and the timeframe extending from the final Passover supper until the crucifixion, the identity of the witness has been established, and his role as the earliest transcriber of the Gospel record made a near certainty.

Inasmuch as this guide does not substitute for the treatise itself, the actual linguistic breakthroughs producing the identity of the witness, must be left to the main body of the work.

Here, I shall indicate that we now can assert with absolute confidence that he was Matthias, the scribal *episkopas*, chosen by Simon/Peter to replace Judas Iscariot as the twelfth Disciple and mentioned only once in the New Testament in Acts I:26.

The investigation

Because John the Baptizer was put to death by Herod Antipas, the tetrarch administering justice in the same region where Jesus lived, the Galilee, and both men were cousins, preaching the imminent Kingdom of God, scrutiny of what John had done which might have similarly motivated the tetrarch to seek Jesus' execution seemed worthy of investigation. Further, the Gospel of Luke records Antipas was present in Jerusalem when Pilate's verdict to crucify Jesus was rendered.

Aside from these common features, the circumstances varied widely: The Gospels record that John the Baptizer was imprisoned by Herod Antipas for "telling him" it was not lawful to have married Herodias, his brother Philip's wife (Luke 3:19-20, Matthew 14:3-4, and Mark 6:17-18).

Josephus strongly implies that John incited the population to take sides against Antipas in an anticipated incursion by the Nabataean king, Aretas IV (Antiquities 18:5:2 "when others massed about John they were very greatly moved by his words. Herod Antipas feared that such strong influence over the people might carry to a revolt...")

Jesus had neither ridiculed the tetrarch for his unlawful (adulterous) marriage, nor had he made seditious speeches aligning himself with the Nabataean warrior king as had John.

Nevertheless, the possibility that Antipas had orchestrated Jesus' crucifixion remained under consideration.

The treatise follows a trail of seemingly fragmented texts, often conjoined to narratives forming an opaque story-line concerning Jesus' months from the time of John's arrest until his execution. It places John's incarceration late 31 to the early winter of 32CE and his execution in the beginning of spring, towards the end of March.

By focusing on texts exploring the deep devotion John the Baptizer and Jesus felt for each other, there could be no doubt John's arrest would be devastating news to Jesus.

At about the time of John's incarceration, several events occur which, upon reassembling Matthias' fragmented text, have now altered previous understanding of what was to befall Jesus.

In the Gospel account, the first appears to be a singular development famously forming the basis of future church apostleship. It is the episode known as "The Sending Out Of the Twelve." Jesus instructs his twelve Disciples they must go to towns and villages without him. And they must spread the word of the Kingdom of God (Matthew 10:7), "...if anyone will not welcome you...it will be more tolerable for the land of Sodom and Gomorrah on the Day of Judgment than for that town..." (Matthew 10:15). (From these much revered words has been promulgated the general emphasis upon Christians to proselytize the faith.)

Shortly thereafter, according to Matthew 11:21 and its parallel Luke 10:13 Jesus reproached the towns, Chorazin, Beit Zaida and Kfar Nahum (Capernaum), which were his preaching, healing and praying domicile, for no other reason than that they did not repent upon witnessing "the deeds of power" he performed in their precincts.

The uncharacteristically harsh "damnation" of these town for not witnessing his deeds of power, have, in the treatise, been reassembled from the Matthias fragments. These are the results:

Jesus' damnation of Beit Zaida, Chorazin and Capernaum (so uncharacteristic for not appreciating his Divine powers, more typically always kept a secret) actually occurs because he has been banished from their town limits. The evidence is that he tells his twelve Disciples they must go to other villages without him, and they must "proclaim the good news the Kingdom of heaven has come near" (Matthew 10:7).

These texts are now returned to their historical sequence for the first time.

In sum:

Jesus was banished from the three towns, perhaps as a public disturbance, expresses his anger (in the form of 'damning' them), and sends away his Disciples.

Where does he go? There is no doubt Jesus spent his time of retreat with Matthias, most probably in his home, located in Ephraim.

Meanwhile, during John's incarceration, the Gospels provide critical information concerning the Disciples' activity. They preached the "Good News" to John's followers that Jesus was God's anointed King of the Jews, saying (Luke 7:18-7:19), "The blind see, the lame walk, lepers are cleansed, the deaf hear...Happy is the one who has faith in Jesus" (Luke 7:23).

In other words, Simon/Peter took the opportunity to establish his leadership in the absence of Jesus, and with John in prison, proselytized the advent of the Kingdom of God, proclaiming: "Jesus, King of the Jews." Ominously, it was the charge over the cross.

While he was residing with Matthias, Jesus was apparently made aware of John's execution, and upon receiving word, departed for the shore of the lake to join John's grieving followers in a memorial gathering on the southern shore of the Sea of Galilee. As they arrived together, a Matthias fragment recorded a famous remark by Jesus, at the sight of John's mournful following, saying they were like "sheep without a shepherd" (Mark 6:34).

As the investigation proceeds, one may wish to keep these certainties in mind: 1. The perpetrator was an individual with political power sufficient to orchestrate a state-sanctioned murder/execution by crucifixion, and 2. that individual had to have brought the charge Jesus had seditiously led people to believe he was "King of the Jews" (carved over the cross).

[Note: Never before unearthed until this author's study, "A Documented Biography of Jesus Before Christianity," was there a memorial gathering at which Jesus offered a eulogy for John and which became a critical event placing Jesus in mortal danger.]

After loudly proclaiming John's greatness, standing as he did by the water's edge to deliver the mournful eulogy (recovered from many of Matthias' fragments and reassembled in the treatise), Jesus refused to let his cousin's criticism of the tetrarch's adulterous marriage be silenced by his state-sanctioned murder. Herodias had married Antipas while still wed to his living half-brother Philip. The Roman civil court might have upheld their conjugal adultery, but John had cited their relationship as contrary to Torah law. So Jesus, refusing to let the voice of his cousin be so ruthlessly muzzled, declared, *"If a woman divorces her husband and then marries another, she commits adultery" (Mark 10:12).*

Any risk of Antipas' contempt for the insult, made known to him by spies present at that memorial gathering, should have been no serious threat, for there was nothing Jesus had done to justify a charge of sedition. Unlike John who encouraged support for an invasion by the Nabataean Aretas, Jesus had crossed no political line.

Then, as he turned to depart by way of Simon/Peter's nearby fishing boat anchored offshore, wading into the small waves, John's followers, hailed him **"King of the Jews"** just as they had come to believe, revering John as their beloved "Elijah" whose role it had been to precede Jesus' coming to usher in the Kingdom–promised and preached by Simon/Peter while he was in prison...but Jesus' departure, perhaps thought to invite a communal Baptism, the crowd surged into the water, forcing Jesus to barely escape their grasping hands as John 6:15 states:

"When Jesus realized the crowd was about to take him by force to make him King (of the Jews), he withdrew...."

Not long after the boat beached in the area of Magdala, the Gospel narrative quotes Herod Antipas as asking his spies who were at the memorial gathering:

"John I beheaded. But who is this about whom I hear such things? (Luke 9:9)

When he was led to believe it was "another John" (who had insulted his marriage as adulterous, and given him the basis for a legitimate capital charge of sedition, with the crowd hailing Jesus, "King of the Jews"), he decided on killing him.

Our evidence is Luke 13:31-32: "At that very hour some Pharisees came and said to him (Jesus), get away from here, for Herod (Antipas) wants to kill you."

Then, reassembling the Matthias' fragment:

"He (Jesus) said to them, 'Go tell that fox for me...I (will) be on my way...(to Jerusalem).'"

With the treatise now having established Antipas' motive (revenge for the insult to his marriage) and opportunity (legal justification owing to the seditious coronation of Jesus as "King of the Jews"), the fact of the tetrarch's guilt remains to be proved.

The treatise, first turns to the actual role of the Jews whose apparent demand for Jesus' crucifixion is analyzed as a historic defamation with no basis in fact.

Generally, a suspect in a murder is asked to produce an "alibi" showing they could not have committed the crime because they were elsewhere, or otherwise incapacitated. In the Gospels, the narrative portrait of crowds of bloodthirsty Jews, including Temple administrators, such as priests and a "council," as well as community leaders, the "scribes, elders and Pharisees," among others are all ghoulishly portrayed as participating in Jesus' final demise.

Therefore, Jewish innocence must be based on alternate evidence than the typical "alibi." The treatise has already indicated that there is sharp variance in the expected recorded testimony of Jews at Caiaphas' hearing, compared to those supposedly clamoring for his crucifixion. These supposedly same groups: chief priests, a "council" and an assembled myriad witnesses, once outside the hearing become free of their prior restraint on giving actual testimony. In fact, as the treatise argues in greater detail, there is no actual testimony by Jews that Jesus ever committed the act of claiming to be "King of the Jews."

Given that is so, does evidence exist that the actual description of the Jews urging Jesus' crucifixion is a work of theological fiction?

Considerable, illuminating deconstruction of the "Barabbas" passages reveal just that fact. Briefly, the characterization of venomous Jews rejecting an offer made by Pontius Pilate to free Jesus as a "traditional" Passover festival gesture of good will, preferring liberation of a murderer named "Barabbas, is blatantly false. First, there is no recorded example of Pilate ever freeing a Jewish prisoner on Passover as an act of political conciliation. Second, there is no such name as "Barabbas." It is a fantasy moniker created as a literary symbol. "Bar-Abbas" actually means: "Son of the father," indicating the Jews preferred to free the son of "their father" (satan) while condemning to die the son of God.

A third analytical observation is of notable relevance: The unique vituperative vocabulary "Crucify him," stands out as a singular malign linguistic element used by the supposedly barbarous crowds, rejecting Pilate's offer to free Jesus (19:6). In that the stylistic idiom is repeated farther on (19:15), its usage exposes the peculiar vernacular as the enhancement of the same editorial fabricator. In other words, given that the "Barabbas" story is utterly false (based on the above criteria) and is a defamation of the Jews as offspring of satan, the subsequent passage portraying Pilate as adjudicating Jesus' fate pending the complicit verdict of Jewish authorities, one concludes the employment of the same idiomatic vocabulary, "crucify him," reveals the subsequent clamor has defamatory intent authored by the same hand as conjured Barabbas. It is all one woven fabric of lies about the Jews, a travesty exposed by constancy of style.

Exactly what the Gospel editors' motive for attributing to a Jewish mob the savage determination to see Jesus crucified, is a subject which awaits the concluding section of the treatise and guide. Here, one observes only, that the Gospels' contempt toward the Jews produced a fictionalized portrait so historic in its defamatory consequence, no blasphemy has infected with its sacrilege atrocities of equal measure.

Part four: Proof that Herod Antipas not only had motive and legal justification for Jesus' crucifixion–but actually did it.

Four central pillars of evidence support an irrefutable verdict condemning the Galilean tetrarch, Herod Antipas, as the orchestrator and perpetrator of Jesus' execution.

Note: This abbreviated guide presents a summary of the historical case against Antipas. The treatise faced a challenge in isolating the more complete record, a full indictment, based on Matthias' syntactically reassembled fragments, which are intertwined with a mixture of anti-Jewish polemical portraits and misleading characterizations of the role played by the two main figures judging Jesus.

One is Pontius Pilate and the other, Herod Antipas.

First, concerning Pilate: A standard reading of the text blames the malevolent Jews for their virulent scorn of Jesus, while regarding Pontius Pilate's acquiescence to the Jews' demand he be crucified as an example of his personal moral morass. Further, Christian doctrine agrees with the Jerusalem governor's "reluctantly" accepting their descendants as eternally responsible for the execution.

Concerning Herod Antipas: Far more obfuscated is his role in the unfolding drama. First, The Galilean tetrarch is only even mentioned as present in Jerusalem in the Gospel of Luke (23:6-16).

One may observe that if he had nothing whatsoever to do with Jesus' arrest and execution, there would be little likelihood of the Gospels inserting him into the unfolding drama. Yet, he is accorded a significant responsibility: Pilate adumbrates his role is to decide/approve Jesus' fate, indicating that authority accrues to him owing to his stature as ruler of the Galilee where Jesus resides ("When Pilate learned Jesus was under Antipas' jurisdiction, he sent him to him" (somewhere in that same vicinity 23:7).

Herod Antipas' possible "alibi" of having been elsewhere is thus eviscerated, as is his claim to having no authority to cause the crucifixion.

All that remains for the verdict to be proved that he perpetrated the crime of murdering Jesus, is to show he was the one who fostered the charge Jesus claimed to be "King of the Jews" and was in Jerusalem to see it was carried out.

Two remarkable acts, one by Herod Antipas and the other by Pontius Pilate are described in the Gospels. Properly understood, they are the key to solving the murder.

Luke 23:11 informs us that when Jesus is brought before Herod Antipas, prior to his judgment by Pontius Pilate (in recognition of his administrative authority as tetrarch of the Galilee), he is mocked as a king with the adornment of a royal robe.

Since we have established that no Jews testified they ever heard Jesus claim that title, and Antipas had only heard about "John's eulogy/anointing ceremony" from spies, his disdain for Jesus as a "fake king" exhibited in the royal robe mockery, had only one possible nexus between that act and the impending judgment by Pilate: his foreknowledge of the charge. Antipas was mocking Jesus for his supposed pretension to being "King of the Jews," proving he was aware of the charge of sedition he was facing.

Having bedecked him in that mock, royal robe prior to Jesus' judgment by Pilate, Antipas demonstrated he knew what the charge over the cross would be. Further, his administrative authority to approve the verdict, as stated by Pontius Pilate, leaves no doubt he did so with awareness and intent. A repetition of the satisfaction he took at avenging the insult to himself and Herodias when John harangued their adulterous marriage, was imminent. Jesus said a woman could not divorce her husband, and he was about to be crucified for his thinking he could be "another John" without suffering the same fate.

Complicating the treatise's assertion of his guilt in perpetrating the murder, were two factors:

1. The Gospels describe Pontius Pilate as also joining his cohort of soldiers in the governor's quarters (the building behind the seat of judgment) and having a "purple" royal robe put on Jesus to mock him as King (John 19:2-4). This is plainly an editorial gloss designed to obfuscate Antipas' original mockery when he, along with his soldiers, is first to adorn him with the robe.

    When Antipas places the royal mantle on Jesus, even its description is transparently altered from the standard purple robe worn by royalty. To divert suspicion from Antipas as the murderer, and make Pilate seem equally if not more complicit in yielding to the ghoulish Jews, a coat described as "elegant" or "bright" (Luke 23:11) is draped over Jesus' frame by Antipas' soldiers in their mockery of him. The intention of the Gospel editor is to suppress doubt Antipas ever knew Jesus was charged with claiming to be King of the Jews, and thereby to free the tetrarch as the object of suspicion he was the actual perpetrator of his state sanctioned murder-on-the cross. Therefore a "purple robe of mockery" is made part of the Pontius Pilate scene as a Lukan coverup, although a Matthias fragment had been retained in the Gospel of John, revealing Antipas was the one seeking Jesus' execution.

2. A second issue for the treatise to resolve was whether Pontius Pilate would have acceded to Herod Antipas' request to crucify Jesus.

Because Herod Antipas and Pontius Pilate were known to dislike each other, the agreement to crucify Jesus was not assuredly a punishment of Jesus carried out at the request of the Galilean tetrarch.

The matter was resolved as follows:

Politically, Herod Antipas was far more valuable to Pontius Pilate as an ally than as a foe. Any misstep or perceived popular unrest the governor/procurator of Jerusalem might cause which was appealed to Vitellius, the Roman legate under whose supervision and constraint he administered Jerusalem, if brought before Emperor Tiberius, could result in his ouster. To have Antipas weigh in on his behalf, testifying his actions, especially in suppressing the Samaritans, were warranted, would be politically invaluable.

So it was (according to the Gospels) that sharing a laugh at the sight of the foolish-looking king, "Antipas and Pilate became friends with each other...for before this they had been enemies" (Luke 23:12).

Part five: What motivated Simon/Peter and the earliest apostles to embellish the Gospel canon with a portrait of Jews "pressing for the death of Jesus" and imbuing them with the "satanic" purpose of wanting to see Christ crucified?

Not lending itself to an abstracted summary of this most central closing message of the treatise, one which marks the culmination of **Responsio Iudaeorum,** I urge the reader to fully consider the document's final argument and insights, and not let this brief summary be a substitute.

According to Mark 8:31 and Luke 9:22, a postmortem interlocution, Jesus speaks to Simon/Peter of his own coming travail, saying, "(I must undergo)...great suffering, and be <u>rejected</u> by the elders, the chief priests and the scribes and be killed and in three days rise again."

The Gospel of Matthew omits mention of "rejection."

Jesus' supposed equating of his "suffering" with his "rejection" by Jewish leaders proves to be the cornerstone of hate and the basis for understanding the bloodthirsty portrait of the Jews permeating the Gospels.

That "rejection" neither before, nor after Jesus' death, became a manifest form of persecution. Never was Jesus subject to suffering for having become the cause of more than marginal public disturbances, perhaps in a local synagogue when he healed on a Shabbat, or argued with Pietists publicly. Prior to his arrest there was one possibly violent confrontation during Hanukkah, but he was not injured. And, in Jerusalem, during the final week, his arrest, hearing, judgment and crucifixion hardly are scenes one would describe as "suffering" due to "rejection."

Simply, there was no exceptional contempt for Jesus or his teaching. According to the archeological evidence, in the first three years following the crucifixion, when the so-called Jerusalem movement was organizing itself to spread "the good news," Jewish rejection took the form of indifference.

Ancient textual evidence of conversions by Jews to the fledgling faith in Jesus as the resurrected Christ is next to non-existent, and there were no Galilean churches built in that three-year interim following his crucifixion.

Taken together, these facts, when linked to the equating of Jesus' "rejection" with his "suffering" lead to a profound conclusion:

> *Traditional Jews were a threat to "kill the faith in Jesus as the Christ" by their simple "REJECTION" of their belief in his Divinity.*

The Gospels' portrayal of Jews conspiring to kill Jesus and participating in his state-sanctioned murder, proves to have been defamation with a theological purpose: to save "Jesus as the Christ" which the influence Jewish rejection of his Divinity threatened to have on prospective proselytes. Evidence suggests Jews as "killers of faith" in Jesus as the Christ, metamorphosed into Gospel ghouls plotting and clamoring for his crucifixion. The textual gore was a literary tactic intended to threaten prospective proselytes with the hovering talons of the Jewish satan, waiting to carry them off. By portraying the Jew as "pressing for the death of Christ" the likely impression the Gospels would make on a new member of the fledgling church was to squelch his temptation to be a traditional Jew, transforming the priests, elders, scribes and "council," along with the clamoring crowd into the bloodthirsty progeny of satan, those who had caused Christ his suffering and upon whom the proselyte's only hope of salvation depended.

ABSTRACT

The Jew has, for millennia, been demonized as a bloodthirsty conspirator in Jesus' crucifixion, portrayed as such in church services and sermons, inviting decent people of faith to liturgically join the reprise of the sacred Gospel Canon, spawning hatred in countless Christian hearts and minds.

Responsio Iudaeorum Nostrae Aetatis investigates the case surrounding Jesus' arrest, hearing, judgment and crucifixion, proving there was no complicity by Jews motivated to silence his teaching, terminate his ministerial activity or prevent his revelation as God's anointed King.

In the course of presenting the investigation's results the treatise first details the general consensus which emerged in 1965 from the Catholic church in a series of dicta known as "Nostra Aetate," an official Vatican II Council decree expressing the sentiment that hate of Jews for their role in the death of Jesus must cease. That position nonetheless maintained as immutable truth the Gospels' canonized portrayal of Jews orchestrating and "pressing for the death of Christ."

Presented in the form of a legal brief, **Responsio Iudaeorum** analyzes the four canonized Gospels' most critical passages accusing Jews, and deconstructing them step-by-step establishes the basis for a complete reassessment of what actually occurred.

Among the major findings:

1. Recovered: The identity of a primary witness for the first time, along with his fragmented scribal entries. Reassembled evidence proves a politically powerful non-Hebrew had a personal motive to kill Jesus.

2. As the true perpetrator is exposed, a heretofore unknown sequence of events occurring in the months prior to the crucifixion is found to have put Jesus in mortal danger and led to his arrest.

3. Concomitantly, Galilean Jews are proved innocent of conspiring or acting to kill Jesus. The explicit accusation "priests, elders, Pharisees, Herodians, scribes, a Temple Council, or a bloodthirsty crowd" sought his death for claiming to be equal to, or the Son of God, or wished him crucified "out of envy" is fully refuted.

The Gospels' portrayal of Jews conspiring to kill Jesus and participating in his state-sanctioned murder, is shown to have been defamation with a theological purpose: to save "Jesus as the Christ" from the influence Jewish rejection of Jesus' Divinity might have on prospective proselytes. Evidence suggests Jews as "killers of faith" in Jesus as the Christ, metamorphosed into Gospel ghouls plotting and clamoring for his crucifixion. The textual gore was a literary tactic intended to threaten prospective converts with the hovering talons of the Jewish satan, waiting to pounce and carry them off.

Responsio Iudaeorum Nostrae Aetatis

A Response from The Jewish People of Our Time Eternally Accused in The Christian Gospels of Conspiring to Kill Jesus

The Case Against the Gospels' False Accusation

A NEW DEFENSE BASED ON RECENT SCHOLARSHIP IN THE MATTER OF HIS ARREST, JUDGMENT AND CRUCIFIXION

Wherefore:

The case shall be made in the fashion of a legal brief, proving there was no complicity in the arrest, hearing, judgment or crucifixion of Jesus by any Jews motivated by their Jewish origins to prevent his revelation as God's anointed King. Nor did any Jews conspire to achieve his demise based on a theological incentive to silence his teaching or terminate his ministerial activity.

The contents of the following document are divided into five parts:

I The Current Status of the Accusation That There Existed a Jewish Conspiracy to Kill Jesus

An investigation divided into four tiers:

II A General Accusation: Passages in the Gospels Manifesting Blame for Jesus' Death

III Identifying the One Who Orchestrated the Pursuit, Capture, Hearing, Judgment and Crucifixion of Jesus

IV The Defense of the Jews

V The Motive for Scapegoating the Jews

I

The Current Status of the Accusation

Opening remarks:

Guided by not only past decades, but centuries, of experience faced personally and as a community, the Jewish People are fully cognizant of the contempt which musters against us owing to the death of Jesus on the cross. Usually the more modern expressions of malice are not identified by graffiti or slogans conjuring descriptions of bloodthirsty priests at the foot of the cross, or the plethora of Gospel and New Testament portraits vilifying Jews as planning Jesus' death. Instead, there is the swastika, or the desecration of a cemetery; worse, in these first decades of the twenty-first century, there has been the mass murder of those praying in synagogues.

Wherever these present themselves: the sight of a skull cap, English spoken with a Yiddish accent, dietary exclusiveness, a name of Jewish origin, practice of Jewish custom, observance of the Shabbat (Sabbath), manner and times of prayer, and those laws expressing recognizably Jewish culture often resulting in separateness from non-Jewish regions of villages, towns, or cities, with outwardly different celebrations of holidays and festivals:

when taken together with our denial of Jesus' Divine origin, the image of the attempted Christ-killer Jew, portrayed in the four canonized Gospels of the New Testament, Matthew, Mark, Luke and John, has awakened in vast numbers of presumably decent, church-going Christians, a faith–indoctrinated certainty our unwitting purpose on earth was to sacrifice the lamb of God, and in causing Jesus' death, accomplish his Divine Plan to take away the sins of mankind, so that even us Jews today, still tainted, shall be forgiven on the day we bear witness to his true identity as God's only Son.

In consonance with church dogma, vast numbers of the faithful have been further led to believe since the time of Luther in the 15th century the Jew has had an agenda to reduce the Christian populace to poverty by a nefarious, conspiratorial scheme to garnish the monetary sustenance of gentiles through manipulation of the world's monetary structure, manifest in excessive interest on loans. To many contemporary Jew-hating Christians, the long-nosed, money-lending banker is a common stereotype borne of this purpose.

In Sum:

The Jew has been liturgically demonized in sanctified church services and sermons, quoting the sacred Gospel Canon, spawning hatred in countless Christian hearts and minds, stimulating vast hordes to carry out crusades of annihilation, build walls of imprisoning ghettoization, conduct inquisitions forcing conversion or death, deporting entire populations into exile, slaughtering the innocent in pogrom massacres and ultimately exterminating millions in the gas chambers of the Holocaust. If the Jew has not been willing to accept Jesus, either forcible conversion or utter elimination have been the means employed to remove our contamination from this world, enticing Jesus to find this earthly domain pure enough for his Second Coming.

Under Pope John XXIII in the early 1960's, to ameliorate what he recognized was the source of hate emerging from the Gospel description of Jewish participation in Jesus' hearing, judgment and crucifixion, the Vatican began a formulary of dicta to guide Catholic thinking toward forgiveness.

Inasmuch as the Pontiff expressed a desire to alter church teachings, we have affirmation the significance of the problem is not disputed. As we shall detail below, subsequent renditions of the Catholic "Nostra Aetate" (literally, "In Our Time"), as the Council edict came to be known, offered no acquittal, only a theological requirement that the future salvation of the Jews through an eventual faith in Jesus, demanded an end by Catholic clergy and the faithful to condemning us as an accursed People beyond redemption. As the formulary evolved, with changes from the year it was first promulgated in 1963 as "Decree on the Jews" (Decretum de Iudaeis) authored by Cardinal Augustin Bea, it early on included text reading:

> **"With unshaken faith and deep longing the Church awaits union with this (Jewish) people. At the time of Christ's coming, a remnant chosen by grace (Rom 11:5). The Church believes, however, with the Apostle that at the appointed time, the fullness of the children of Abraham according to the flesh will embrace him who is salvation (Rom 11:12, 26). Their acceptance will be life from the dead (see: Rom 11:15)."**

In August, 1965 the Vatican II Document was altered to preserve the role of the Jews as having been deicidal in the manner described in the Gospels. The textual variant with the alteration was as follows:

> **"True, the Jewish authorities and those who followed their lead pressed for the death of Christ: still, what happened in his passion cannot be charged against all the Jews, without distinction, then alive, nor against the Jews of today....It is wrong to call the (Jews) an accursed people, since they remain very dear to God... since the Lord, by his passion and death, washes away the sins of all men, which were the cause of the passion and death of Jesus Christ (Luke 23:34; Acts 3:17; 1 Cor. 2:8)."**

> **"...All should see to it that, in catechetical work and in the preaching of the word of God, they teach nothing save what conforms to the truth of the gospel and the spirit of Christ. In her rejection of injustice of whatever kind and wherever inflicted upon men, mindful of that common patrimony, the council decries and condemns hatreds and persecutions directed against Jews whether they arose in former or in our own days. All should see to it that, in catechetical work and in the preaching of the word of God, they teach nothing that could give rise to hatred of Jews in the hearts of Christians."**

Removed from this final text were the following words: "The Jewish people never should be represented as rejected or accursed, or guilty of deicide."

Of importance is this document's intention to establish the basis for a genuine ecumenical reconciliation between Jews and Christians.

However, the very concept of "Jews being forgiven" pending salvation, amounts to an accusation re-stated in terms supposedly less pejorative than "satanic" and commensurately less progenitive of hate. It amounts to reaffirming that the Jews sought and abetted the death of Jesus, but shall find grace at the End of Days, and therefore must not be despised in our own time, *nostra aetate.*

None of us, whether Jews or Christians, should underestimate the spiritual commitment we make to beliefs nurturing our lives and faith. For untold centuries, Christianity made such a venerable, revered choice embedded in the circumstances of its origins, decreeing that the crucifixion began a new Covenant of Jesus' followers with Christ, replacing God's Covenant with Abraham.

In recent years, the question of whether the Covenant with Abraham had been superseded by the crucifixion, and whether such a doctrine is a theology of the Catholic Church became the subject of debate between Pope Emeritus Benedict XVI and the Chief Rabbi of Vienna, who quoted early Catholic dicta on the subject, indicating the Covenant of the Crucifixion had replaced that of Abraham.

The Gospel message is clear. Even colored by apostolic enhancement, the text of Luke 16:16 explicitly states that with John the Baptist's arrival, Torah was replaced by preaching the Kingdom of God. The shift from the endpoint of the Abrahamic Covenant occurring with John's doctrinal role, to the crucifixion, is evidenced by the Matthew 27:51-53, describing the End of Days scenario coinciding with Jesus' death: The earth shaking, tombs opening, and the resurrection of "many saints." These were the supposed signs that the Torah's Covenant with Abraham, and the Torah itself were "finished" (based on Jewish tradition which Jesus had taught, Matthew 5:18). The Gospel interprets Jesus' utterance from the cross, "It is finished," to mean "The purpose of the Torah has been fulfilled," and with it the Abrahamic Covenant (John 19:28-30). The new Covenant of the Crucifixion, ushered in by the utterance: "It is finished/fulfilled" marked the advent of the replacement of Abraham's Covenant and was joined by those with faith the crucifixion heralded the Kingdom of God.

From its inception as a fledgling church, the theological diminution of the Abrahamic Covenant was a necessary formula for dispensing with any constraints on massacres and forced conversions or the ghettoization of Jews, perfidies in the service of Christ, avenging his crucifixion which supposedly had been enabled by Jews. If the Church had truly continued to venerate the Covenant with Abraham (as Pope Benedict XVI erroneously claimed) the atrocities in the name of Christ could never have been theologically justified.

Today, the term "Judeo-Christian" has become, to the trained ear, a "supersessionist" (from "supersede") code term. It indicates that one day, presumably when Jesus returns as the Christ for all to bear witness, Judaism shall be fully "superseded" by Christianity and vanish as a religion.

In other words, what the term "Judeo-Christian disguises, as if there is a comfortable stasis in the relationship, is actually, the prophesied future arrival of Jesus as the Son of God, and the migration of "Judeo" into a final, apocalyptic merger when its identity shall be one with Christ.

As Jesus taught: (Matthew 12:33 and 7:17) "The tree is known by its fruit...but the bad tree bears bad fruit."

Plainly, Nostra Aetate's intent has been to ameliorate the Gospel-provoked hate of the Jews. But the "Crucifixion Covenant" (terminating God's Covenant with Abraham) and more modern forms of felonious theology, formulating a doctrine of Christ as superseding Judaism, the latter to be dispensed with–comprises no element of acquittal for participating in Jesus' execution.

Now we of the DEFENSE ask that Christians of genuine good-will join us as we investigate and expose the circumstances and evidence genuinely acquitting us.

As our investigation proceeds, and follows a course altogether departing from church doctrine, we deeply commiserate with the travail Jesus suffered, and share a sense of profound loss that his spiritual voice as a teacher of righteousness communicating faith in a future of love between all people was silenced by murder on the cross.

RESPONSUM IN BEHALF OF ALL JEWISH PEOPLE SO ACCUSED

WHEREAS:

"To teach nothing save what conforms to the truth of the Gospel" is a mandate of the Vatican II Dicta, our response begins with words and summarized sentiments based on indicated Gospel and New Testament passages containing an **accusation** of the Jews:

II

A General Accusation Based on the Gospels

During Jesus' ministry, Jews in the region of the Galilee and Judea, "Pharisees, Herodians, Priests, Scribes, Elders and Council members" (mentioned at different junctures) became incensed by his equating himself with God, manifest in the performance of miracles, healings, forgiveness of sins of those beseeching his touch, and pronunciations concerning his own identity as the Son of God, and sought to kill him. Those Jews who conspired to bring about his arrest and ultimate crucifixion were acting from an envious nature, borne of their own unsuspected purpose, to enable Jesus' body be transformed from mortal death to rule all mankind from heaven as the anointed King of the Jews and all mankind.

Passages in the Gospels manifesting blame for Jesus' death
(annotated with occasional DEFENSE objections,
all to be elaborated farther on)

From Matthew: 12:14 with a parallel in Mark 3:6
According to the Gospel description, Jesus entered a synagogue on Shabbat (the Sabbath), and was approached by a man with a withered hand to be healed. The text states "they" (presumably the Jewish

10

congregants) and Pharisees (3:6) who were present, "watched him to see if he would cure him on the Shabbat so they might accuse him."

The text continues, following the healing, which suggests Jesus overruled Torah law by conducting the healing:

"The Pharisees went out and conspired against him, how to destroy him." (Matthew 12:14)

In Mark 3:6 a slight, but significant variation occurs: The Gospel text reads, "The Pharisees went out and conspired with the *Herodians* against him, how to destroy him."

Most likely, the Herodians were Galilean Jews who favored the adulterous marriage between Herod Antipas and Herodias, despite her never receiving a divorce from her husband Philip, Antipas' living half-brother. These so-called Herodians had supported their wedlock because Herodias was a descendant of the famed Maccabees and could become a Jewish queen were the tetrarch granted the title, king. Therefore, one may reason, Antipas rewarded them with membership in the Tiberius municipal council, and they thus earned the name "Herodians."

In text taken from John:

Chapter 5:1-16 details a miraculous cure of a blind man, stating "Therefore the Jews started persecuting Jesus because he was doing such things (as healing) on the Sabbath." Added to this is the text: "For this reason the Jews were seeking all the more to kill him (for) also calling God his own father...(John 5:18).

John 7:1 states simply: Jesus could not stay in Judea (the south) but only in the Galilee, because "The Jews were out to kill him."

In a passage which Christianity refers to as the "First Prediction of the Passion" (Matthew:16:21; Mark 8:31; Luke 9:22), Jesus is quoted as telling the Disciples: "(He must go to Jerusalem) and undergo great suffering, and be rejected/at the hands of the elders, chief priests and scribes, and be killed...."

And John 11:49-11:50 has Caiaphas meet with the chief priests and Pharisees, when he says, "It is better for you that one man should die on behalf of the people than the whole nation..."

The frequent passages portraying Jews as adversaries of Jesus, particularizing their community as differentiated from him by laws and mores contrary to the universal Kingdom of God, culminate in the scenes of his hearing, judgment and crucifixion.

In Matthew 26:57, after Jesus has been arrested, it is written, he was "taken to Caiaphas the High Priest in whose house the scribes and the elders had gathered..." (The text notes that Simon/Peter went only as far as the exterior courtyard, 26:69, not going inside the house. This matches John 18:16).

Matthew 26:59 continues: "Now the chief priests and the whole council were looking for false testimony against Jesus so that they might put him to death, though they found none, though many false witnesses came forward."

Mark 14:55-56 reads: "the chief priests and whole council were looking for testimony against Jesus to put him to death, but they found none...many gave false testimony against him and their testimony did not agree."

To those Gospel editors accusing the Jews of wanting to see Jesus crucified, the "false testimony" evokes the rabid anger of witnesses attempting to say what was necessary to see him found guilty and executed. Even if they did not have any evidence against him, they would turn Jesus' innocence to guilt.

Both the Gospels of Matthew (26:59) and Mark (14:55) state:

"The chief priests and whole council were looking for false testimony against Jesus so that they might put him to death. But they found none.

Matthew continuing:

"Though many false witnesses came forward."

Mark continuing:

"For many gave false testimony against him and their testimony did not agree."

As we shall see just below, once Jesus is taken before Pilate for judgment, the Gospel of Luke does have the witnesses seeming to recall his seditious crimes warranting crucifixion, as they testify (23:2-5): "We found this man perverting our nation, forbidding us to pay taxes to the emperor, and saying he himself is the messiah, a king."

At his hearing, before they bind and lead him away to Pilate, even Caiaphas seems confused when there is no such accusation, saying (Matthew 26:63-64), "I put you under oath before the living God. Tell us if you are the Messiah (anointed one=King of the Jews). Jesus said to him, 'You have said so.'"

Upon hearing this, Caiaphas demands of the gathering,

"Why do we still need witnesses? You have now heard his blasphemy! (presumably, expressed by Jesus' words, "You have said so").

What is your verdict?

They answered, 'He deserves death.'" (Matthew 26:65-66)

[Note: In Mark 14:62 Jesus answered Caiaphas' question, "Are you the Messiah, the son of God," saying, "I am." Had this been historically an un-doctored response, no doubt the other Gospels and all Christianity would have exalted the moment as one of his holiest revelations. Instead it is the apparent relic of the Lukan version:

13

"He said to them you say that I am," and so intentionally retains the misleading affirmation which conceals by omission (i.e. "you say that") his full reply (Luke 22:70).]

According to the four Canonical Gospels, Jesus was then led away to stand judgment before the governor of Jerusalem, Pontius Pilate (Matthias 27:2 and //'s).

In Matthew and Mark the chief priests and elders, now supposedly present at the judgment before the procurator/governor "accuse Jesus"–but the specifics of their accusations are not cited.

In Luke (23:2) "They" presumably refers to accusing chief priests and elders, although mention of the "whole council bringing him before Pilate" (Luke 23:1) is made as well. There is also a suggestion that "crowds" were present (Luke 23:4).

In Matthew (27:11and //'s), Pilate immediately asks Jesus: "Are you King of the Jews?"

In response to the question (Luke 23:3), "Are you the King of the Jews?" Jesus replies, as in the other Gospels, including John (18:37) "You say so."

Beyond those words, "You say so," the Gospels of Matthew 27:14 and Mark 15:5 state: "Jesus gave no answer/made no further reply."

Only in Luke do the witnesses once again add in their testimony to Pilate (23:2):

"We found this man perverting our nation, forbidding us to pay taxes to the emperor, and saying that he himself is the Messiah, a king (23:5)….He stirs up the people, teaching throughout all Judea, from Galilee where he began, even to this place."

[Note: In the section to follow, wherein a systematic analysis of the interrogation is made, a remark by Jesus shall be recalled, which is recorded in Luke 22:67-68: "They said, 'If you are the Messiah, tell us.' He replied, 'If I tell you, you will not believe. And if I question you, you will not answer.'"]

According to the Gospels, Pontius Pilate was only swayed reluctantly toward crucifixion. He is quoted in the texts as saying: "I find no basis for a charge against this man" (Luke 23:4); "Pilate, wanting to release Jesus asked, 'Why what evil has he done? I have found in him no ground for the sentence of death...'" (Luke 3:22) but then acquiescing to the large gathering of Jews comprising Temple priests, council elders, and a clamoring crowd determined Jesus be crucified, he sought a seeming last way out trying to avoid rendering the verdict of death on the cross.

He suggested the Jews overcome their supposed envy of Jesus (Mark 15:10 states "For he realized it was out of jealousy that the chief priests had handed him over") and as was customary on Passover he would release a Jewish prisoner as a token of good will, suggesting it be their "King of the Jews."

"But the chief priests and elders persuaded the crowds (Matthew 27:26) to ask for Barabbas (an insurrectionist and murderer) and to have Jesus killed." So the Jews chose the one named Barabbas, and in reply to Pilate's question about what he should do to Jesus, "Shouted back (Mark 15:12) crucify him!" and "they kept urgently demanding with loud shouts that he be crucified" (Luke 23:23).

The Gospel of Matthew (27:19) offers a reason for Pontius Pilate's otherwise untypical, merciful side. His wife informed Pilate, while he was deciding the verdict, that he should "have nothing to do with that innocent man," because, she explained, she has had a disconcerting dream about him.

When the Jews failed to accept Jesus' release, demanding instead his crucifixion, but asking freedom for Barabbas, Pontius Pilate said

(Matthew 27:24), "I am innocent of this man's blood...then the People as a whole answered, 'his blood be on us and on our children!'"

In all four Gospels, Jesus is then dressed as a mock king in a purple royal robe wearing a crown of thorns and struck on the head with a reed, whereupon the guards knelt before him saying, "hail King of the Jews" all the while slapping and spitting on him.

In the Gospel of John 19:7 the Jews replied to Pilate when he asked what Jesus had done which is a crime deserving crucifixion, "We have a law, and according to that law...he should die because he has claimed to be the Son of God."

Prior to the Jews insisting on the demise of Jesus on the cross, the Gospel of Luke provides an especially vivid and unique passage (23:6-16). In descriptive detail, the tetrarch ruling the Galilee, Herod Antipas, makes an appearance.

"When Herod (Antipas, the Galilean tetrarch) saw Jesus...the chief priests and scribes stood by vehemently accusing him...Herod treated him with contempt and mocked him...then put an elegant robe on him. That same day Herod and Pilate became friends with each other. Before this they had been enemies."

The passages state categorically Herod Antipas was given administrative control over the fate of Jesus since he was a Galilean and came under Antipas' legal authority. The verdict to crucify Jesus was, nevertheless, not rescinded by a decision of the tetrarch, although Pontius Pilate decreed, "Neither has Herod (found this man guilty) for he sent him back to us" (Luke 23:15).

Although the passage begins with Herod Antipas supposedly situated somewhere in Jerusalem, other than in the presence of Pontius Pilate, based on the contradictory descriptions, he was in the building doorway, observing the proceeding from just behind the stone "Gabbatha" courtyard of judgment, perhaps just within the so-called "Praetorium" headquarters.

The royal purple robe was put on Jesus during the scene of judgment by Pilate, not elsewhere in Jerusalem (Matthew 27:28 and Mark 15:17); Yet, Luke 23:10 states the robe mocking him as king was actually put on him by Herod Antipas, and then, only later, did Pilate's cohort "enter" the Praetorium" and put the robe on him.

In fact, the passage which states Antipas demonstrated his verdict Jesus was innocent by sending "him back to us," was obviously a fabrication. Here's a closer look:

Following the mockery by Herod Antipas, when Jesus is flogged and scourged, then verbally and physically abused as a mock king, all by his guards and soldiers (Luke 23:11), he supposedly "sent him back" from somewhere in Jerusalem–but was transparently conveyed by Antipas' soldiers from the courtyard of the Praetorium, where he had, as the evidence shall show, already been adorned in Antipas' royal purple robe in contravention to the treatment of any innocent man. Finally, Pilate reluctantly gives in to the ghoulish crowd, including priests and scribes, shouting, "Crucify him. Crucify him" (John 19:6).

Pontius Pilate's recorded attempt to crucify a murderous infidel named Barabbas instead of Jesus, as a gesture of good will on Passover, does not placate the bloodthirsty Jews who refuse to accept any substitute for God's Son.

Forced to carry the cross, Jesus is aided by a passerby recruited by the Roman guard, a Cyrene named Simon, with no bloodthirsty Jews portrayed (Matthew 27:32 and //'s). Nor is there any angry crowd following him and none of size except female mourners bewailing his fate (Luke 23:27).

On the high hill of crucifixion known as Golgotha, the grim scene of his slowly expiring is accompanied by scribes and elders (Matthew 27:41) chief priests (Mark 15:31-32) and Jewish leaders (Luke 23:35) taking solace from the misery he suffers, portrayed as a visual cause for taunting and making jokes at his supposed claim to be "King of the Jews," the charge for which he is crucified, stated on the cross along with his residential origin as a Nazarene.

III

Identifying the One Who Orchestrated the Capture, Hearing, Judgment and Crucifixion of Jesus

Opening argument:

The murder of Jesus, as the Vatican formally pronounced in 1965, has been largely blamed on:

"The Jewish authorities pressing for the death of Christ"

Considered an act of Jewish instigation and prerogative, preserved as sacred doctrine by the Gospel texts quoted above, chief priests, the "council," scribes, elders and crowds are vividly portrayed joining the clamor to crucify Jesus out of envy (Mark 15:10), and for equating himself with God (John 19:7; Luke 23:2).

All but blameless in these horrific passages, a dispassionate Roman governor, Pontius Pilate, reluctantly yields to the demands of the Temple leadership and populace. Herod Antipas, tetrarch of the Galilee, present in the vicinity according to the Gospel of Luke, in accord with Pilate's verdict, likewise acquiesces to the Jewish demand to crucify Jesus.

Forthwith, the calumnious accusation that Jews felt such seething contempt toward Jesus due to their religious or historical identity, they therefore advocated his murder, shall be fully proved a monstrous libel deserving to be abhorred by all people of conscience.

The DEFENSE shall present newly recovered evidence concerning the actual sequence of events leading to the crime, exposing the actual perpetrator and motive for the murder. This document shall be referred to as: **"Responsio Iudaeorum Nostrae Aetatis"** ("From the Jewish People of Our Time") or more simply as **"Responsio Iudaeorum"** or, "the treatise."

We begin by establishing an altogether new perspective on this topic which has been so closely examined over the past two centuries by theologians and scholars.

Quite unfettered by the Christological agendas of faith-indoctrinated scholars, truth has been recently finding its way to the surface of the heavily-enhanced Gospel text. Recorded and largely fragmented, only to emerge in these times, restored, segmented texts are herein submitted as evidence of the testimony of the *episkopas*, chosen by Simon/Peter as the Twelfth Disciple to replace Judas Iscariot (Acts I:21).

Our DEFENSE shall, as that testimonial record now re-assembled becomes syntactically clear and irrefutably relevant, draw upon the evidence it provides to both convict the true perpetrator of the murder of Jesus, and fully acquit the Jews of any inclination or active participation in his pursuit, capture, forced hearing, judgment, or crucifixion.

The DEFENSE introduces: <u>Matthias,</u> who had accompanied the Disciples when they were with Jesus, and who was always his companion from the time he was baptized by John until he was crucified.

<u>Instances and evidence of his actual presence:</u>

In the Gospel Matthew 26:17 at the last meal known in Christian tradition as the "Last Supper" an individual favored by Jesus sat at his side.

The leading Disciple, Simon/Peter, to whom he was known, asked him who Jesus meant would betray him (John 13:24). That individual, beloved by Jesus, according to the passage, leaned against him in a comradely fashion to inquire, and we are aware Jesus and he were exceptionally trusting of each other, though he is never named. Our assertion herein tendered, with argument for its veracity to follow, is that that person was the same individual referred to shortly thereafter, still unnamed, but of central importance as a witness. He was:

a. At Jesus' side during the group's retreat after the dinner to the Garden of Gethsemane bearing witness to Jesus' prayer not to die, later making record of much of that scene, while Simon/Peter and the others were off at a distance (Matthew 26:36).

b. Present as a witness to the proceedings and interrogation in the House of Annas and Caiaphas the High Priest (Mathew 26:57).

c. In attendance at Gabbatha before Pontius Pilate when Jesus was judged, mocked and led to Golgotha carrying his cross to the site of crucifixion (Matthew 27:11).

d. A sole witness among those of his devotees at the foot of the cross during the crucifixion (Matthew 27:45; John 19:26).

Our evidence that he was the individual upon whose testimony of these events the Gospels' descriptive record depends, are as follows:

One, he is described as having an especially close relationship to Jesus ("the Disciple Jesus loved") and these four events happen in close temporal proximity to each other. Therefore, to suggest there was another unnamed, equally important individual actively attempting to intercede in Jesus' behalf, or providing comfort as a friend, during his time of most severe tribulation tests credulity.

Two, no member of the group of Disciples is indicated in the Gospels as one whose testimony and witnessed account form the basis for the canonized version of the above four events as they are retold from the Last Supper through the Crucifixion. Only one individual, variously referred to as "the 'Disciple Jesus loved,'"(John 13:23) or, "the Disciple," (John 18:15-16) is a nameless protagonist whose role is of supreme relevance to each of the indicated critical moments in the unfolding drama.

Three, this individual is known personally to the High Priest and is described in the Gospel of John as therefore having access to the hearing deciding Jesus' fate. Simon/Peter is without such authority and permitted only by virtue of knowing the unnamed individual to enter just the exterior courtyard of Caiaphas' house where he warmed himself by the fire alongside the servants (Luke 22:55).

Four, in the Gospel of John, the unnamed, beloved individual is said to be present at the crucifixion (John 19:26-27).

[NOTE: Critical re-translation and syntactical reconstruction of the above lines from John provide a significant advance in understanding the actual circumstance. Jesus was, in fact, asking "the Disciple he loved" whom we have identified as our primary witness to so much of this tragedy, to take care *not* of his mother Mary–for she was not there, at the cross, and no other Gospels suggest she

22

was–but to take care of his "nakedness" implying Matthias see he be wrapped in the traditional burial shroud. The Greek words for "woman" and "nakedness" are nearly identical–"gune/gumnos."]

Five, only one individual had the authority of a scribe, was devoted to Jesus and kept in his company through much of his last year or two (if not longer) and was familiar to the twelve Disciples. His relationship with Jesus, according to Peter (Acts I:21-26) was as one who "having accompanied us men from all the time Jesus went in among us and went out from the Baptism by John until the day when he was taken up *to become a witness* (my italics)..." should be therefore chosen as the twelfth Disciple to fill the place left vacant by Judas Iscariot.

From his own words, Simon/Peter has attested he knew the name "Matthias." He also knew Jesus stayed with him and he surely understood how important Matthias would be as a member of the Temple constellation of authorities, and perhaps the administration itself, to nurturing the new church. Based on Simon/Peter's own testimony in Acts I that Matthias was with Jesus all the time, he was the witness described above.

Six, final proof of the above assertion that Matthias' was the unnamed "Disciple Jesus loved" at the Last Supper, the hearing before Caiaphas, the judgment scene at Gabbatha, and at the foot of the cross, occurs in a concluding passage in the Gospel of John quoting Simon/Peter who states "the Disciple's" role was to make a record of the events and bear witness to them, as this treatise claims.

(John 21:20; 21:24):

Simon/Peter (selectively) **"turning and seeing the Disciple whom Jesus loved...the one who had reclined next to Jesus at the supper"** (said) **"This is the disciple who is testifying to these**

23

things and has written them. And we know that his testimony is true..."

The historical setting:

The date of Jesus' arrest has been a matter of continuing debate. The subject is one which compels lengthy argument and does not altar the defense. Hypothetically, based on Jesus' teaching formulations, that Hebrew New Year, Rosh Hashanah and month of Tishri corresponded to the Roman 31 CE, a Sabbatical year, when Jesus, like all rabbis, emphatically urged followers to free all members of the community from grudges and debt.

When Herod the Great died some 36 years earlier, the principality of Judea was reduced to a province of Rome and divided into three administrative regions. For the first ten years after his death, during the reign of Augustus, the city of Jerusalem and its larger environs, called Judea, including Samaria, Jericho, Sebaste and Idumea, were ruled by Herod's son Archelaus, until he was ousted and replaced by Roman governors, also known as procurators, in 6 CE.

The other two regions were ruled by Herod the Great's sons, Antipas and Philip, as "tetrarchs." The former administered the Galilee and Peraea. The two regions were not contiguous, but were separated by an autonomous area of ten independent small towns known as the "Decapolis." Peraea extended southward past Jerusalem forming a border on one side with the Dead Sea, and the country of Nabataea on the other.

Herod Antipas' half brother, the tetrarch Philip, was ruler of Caesaria Philipi and towns and villages in the north, known as the "Hauran." It is a region that spanned parts of southern Syria and northern Jordan.

The murder (or execution) of John the Baptizer

In any murder investigation, comparing the crime with others known to have similar characteristics occurring in the same region and timeframe is a standard procedure.

John, like Jesus, preached the imminent coming of God's Kingdom. He was put to death by the ruler administering justice in the region where Jesus resided, the Galilee.

His execution was carried out upon the order of Herod Antipas, the same tetrarch of the Galilee who the Gospel of Luke records was present in Jerusalem when Pilate's verdict to crucify Jesus was given.

What was the motive for the state "murder" of John the Baptizer? And does it shed light on the ultimate pursuit and arrest of Jesus in Jerusalem? The DEFENSE shall begin with an inquiry into that question.

The Gospels record that John the Baptizer was imprisoned by Herod Antipas for "telling him" it was not lawful to have married Herodias, his brother Philip's wife (Luke 3:19-20, Matthew 14:3-4, and Mark 6:17-18).

According to Torah law, a Roman divorce (which Herodias would have received) was not valid according to Hebrew stricture. Because her husband, Philip was still alive and had never given her his consent, she was an adulteress, and the tetrarch was an adulterer.

(The original intent of this law was to prevent a man from arbitrarily sending a wife away without her promised post-marital security in land holdings, etc.) Therefore, the ancient Hebrew court demanded the husband formally honor those payments through a legal proceeding, granting her the divorce with circumstances the later rabbis delineated often in her favor.

[Note: Scholarship is divided on the identity of Herodias' husband, Philip. A consensus exists he was a son of Herod the Great, had married Herodias, and she had left him to marry her husband's half-brother, the tetrarch, Herod Antipas, without Philip ever having given her a Jewish divorce.

The doubt arises as to whether her husband was Philip the tetrarch (whose mother was Cleopatra II of Jerusalem), or another son of Herod the Great, called Herod II (born to Miriammne, a daughter of a High Priest but also having the name Philip). John's rebuke would have targeted the adulterous marriage in either case.]

Herodias was herself an orphaned daughter of one of Herod the Great's sons, Aristobolus IV, and so was of Maccabean lineage.

Josephus strongly implies that John incited the population to take sides against Antipas in an anticipated incursion by the Nabataean king, Aretas IV (Antiquities 18:5:2 "when others massed about John they were very greatly moved by his words, Herod, who feared that such strong influence over the people might carry to a revolt – for they seemed ready to do anything he should advise –believed it much better to move now than later have it raise a rebellion and engage him in actions he would regret.")

And so John, out of Herod's suspiciousness, was sent in chains to Machaerus, the fort previously mentioned, and there put to death.

(As a historic footnote, several years after Jesus' crucifixion, the famed Arab warrior would lead his camel brigades across the border of Peraea, into Antipas' region to avenge his daughter, Phaesalas' humiliation. As Antipas' Arab wife, she had been forced to flee in dishonor when Herodias moved in.)

Although the Galilee was home to a large community of hyper-observant Jews, a branch of Pharisees properly labeled, "Pietists" (Hebrew: "Hasidim" linking them to a probable genealogy from Maccabean times), among their number were a group who supported Antipas' marriage. They did so hoping Antipas would be elevated by Rome to become a king, as was his father, and Herodias, given her Maccabean lineage, might be a Jewish queen. These Galilean Jews, one may surmise, whom the Gospels group with other northern Pharisees (as noted earlier) were called, "Herodians" because Antipas, it appears, rewarded them with a role in his Tiberius council.

John, according to the Gospels (Mark 6:17-18) was arrested for castigating Herodias' Torah-forbidden, adulterous marriage to Antipas. But the fate which awaited him, his execution, required he be found guilty of sedition against the Empire. Only because he was judged to have incited crowds to rise up militarily against Antipas, hailing the imminent revenge of Aretas IV as punishment by God for Herodias' adultery, had he committed an act of sedition.

Aside from John the Baptizer and Jesus both suffering the fate of state "murders" disguised as legal executions, either under direct orders from or in the presence of the Galilean tetrarch, the two spiritual leaders do not seem to have invited charges for similar offenses.

Jesus had not been known to insult Herodias as an adulteress. And, although the charge for which he was crucified, carved over the cross, read "Jesus of Nazareth King of the Jews," no witnesses at the hearing in Caiaphas' house testified they ever heard him say such a thing about himself.

Nevertheless, to dismiss the possibility that Herod Antipas, who had the authority to sway Pilate's decision (Luke 23:7), did not orchestrate Jesus' crucifixion, would be premature.

John and Jesus

When one discerns the deep affection John and Jesus felt for each other, it is impossible to imagine Jesus was not only saddened, but angered by the grievous injustice of his arrest.

It hardly tests credibility to suggest Jesus ultimately did or said something to avenge the Baptist's death which has never been known, but which caused him to become an enemy of Antipas.

Before investigating how Jesus reacted to John's death, we must be fully cognizant of their shared devotion, one to the other.

Because John "the Baptizer" was Mary's cousin (being the son of Elizabeth, who was the sister of Mary's mother Anna) and so too was Jesus' cousin, only once removed, their family ties were strengthened into an unbreachable spiritual bond as they shared the effort to purify their followers' hearts, with God's Kingdom believed imminent.

The family nexus first becomes apparent in the Gospels when Mary arrived at Elizabeth's home and confided that she was pregnant. We learn Elizabeth would give birth to John in only three more months (Luke 1:36), a prelude to their subsequent, famed interaction, Jesus' own baptism by John.

For the purpose of this investigation, John's immersing his cousin (Matthew 3:14-15) confirms his apparent devotion to Jesus and the depth of their mutual high regard.

A scene (John 3:22-29) somewhat farther along in the Gospels' version of events when both Jesus' Disciples and John's followers join in a festive swim at Aenon, a group purification with spirited "dunking," further reflects the warm feelings and familiarity Jesus and John enjoyed.

Not long after John's arrest, Jesus, apparently criticizing those who had belittled John because of his annoying ("gnat-like") diatribes against the adulterous marriage, rebuked them, saying, "You strain out a gnat but swallow a camel…" (Matthew 23:24)

His remarks were targeting Herodian loyalists who cared more, it seemed about John's harangues against the tetrarch's adultery, than the consequence of that illicit marriage being an imminent invasion by the Arab warrior king, Aretas IV, known as, "the Camel," to avenge his humiliated daughter.

As our investigation proceeds, we have reached the time when John had been incarcerated. While he was in the Macherus prison, the following transpired:

According to Matthew 11:21 and its parallel Luke 10:13 Jesus reproached the towns, Chorazin, Beit Zaida and Kfar Nahum (Capernaum), which were his preaching, healing and praying domicile, for no other reason than that they did not repent upon witnessing "the deeds of power" he performed in their precincts.

Therefore, in what one must certainly acknowledge seems an uncharacteristically harsh expression of condemnation, Jesus curses them with the prospect of their future damnation.

More than likely, the undisguised cause of Jesus' anger finds expression in the prior Gospel passage, in which he tells his twelve Disciples they must go to towns and villages without him. And they must spread the word of the Kingdom of God (Matthew 10:7), "...if anyone will not welcome you...it will be more tolerable for the land of Sodom and Gomorrah on the Day of Judgment than for that town..." (Matthew 10:15).

The curse upon the three towns, expressed as "more tolerable for the land of Sodom and Gomorrah" which Jesus is thought to extend again to the same towns to which his twelve Disciples would go off carrying his message of God's imminent Kingdom, hardly seems to have been a likely repeated phrase, a message to them, should their attempt to enter those same towns prove futile.

We recognize how contrary to Jesus' model of love this expression of anger over personal disregard was and recover the following truer account:

Based on fragmented Gospel text, re-positioned to restore the linkage of events, our investigation posits Matthew 11:21 should be reversed to precede 10:1. Then, the "Sending Away of the Twelve Disciples" on a mission of spreading word about God's coming Kingdom, follows the "cursing" of the three villages.

The result is clarifying:

A.

Chorazin, Beit Zaida and Kfar Nahum (Capernaum), the objects of Jesus' denunciation were targeted NOT for their arrogance, denying his miracles, but because they refused him entry into their environs due to his healings on Shabbat (the Sabbath), perhaps his public disturbances, or as a known associate of John the Baptizer, incarcerated by Antipas, the tetrarch. The passage which uses the identical phrase, cursing the towns which had refused him entry, suggesting their fate would be as "Sodom and Gomorrah" apprises us of the rejection he experienced when his circle was maligned by the inhabitants of those towns, refusing to extend them a welcome.

THEREFORE:

B.

AS A CONSEQUENCE OF NOT BEING PERMITTED ENTRY INTO THE THREE LAKESIDE VILLAGES, CHORAZIN, BEIT ZAIDA AND KFAR NAHUM, JESUS SENT AWAY HIS TWELVE DISCIPLES TO BE ON THEIR OWN.

To authors of the Vatican II 1965 Edict, and Christian faithful the world-over, the "Sending Away of the Twelve" assuredly resonates as a moment when Jesus indicates his messianic message is to be spread by the universal church and has nothing to do with his condemning the three villages. To recognize the "Sending Away of the Twelve" was initiated and caused by Jesus' ostracism by the three lakeside villages is a significant step in discerning the next circumstances in this tragedy.

HERE IS WHAT THE TWELVE DID DURING THEIR TIME ON THEIR OWN DURING JOHN'S INCARCERATION:

They preached the "Good News" to John's followers that Jesus was God's anointed King of the Jews, saying (Luke 7:18-7:19), "The blind see, the lame walk, lepers are cleansed, the deaf hear...Happy is the one who has faith in Jesus" (Luke 7:23).

[As noted: Matthias' recorded Gospel accounts have been obfuscated by disjunctive fragmentation, which when reconstructed return each fragment to syntactical clarity. Taking the text of the Gospel literally, Jesus' Disciples are actually not mentioned. John, upon hearing of Jesus' miracle healings while in jail, supposedly sends his own Disciples to ask Jesus whether he is the Messiah. And Jesus tells John's disciples to report back to the Baptist concerning the wondrous signs he has performed, proving he is the one sent to usher in God's Kingdom.]

Reassembled from Matthias' syntax, that word of his Messiahship was actually spread by Simon/Peter and the Disciples while the Twelve were "sent away" on their own, and Jesus was in retreat.

Charged with sedition for his harangues against Antipas in support of Aretas IV, John was executed, a punishment, certainly meted out to avenge the insult to the tetrarch's wife Herodias, whom the Baptist castigated as an adulteress for marrying his living half-brother, without a Jewish divorce (Mark 6:17-19).

Where was Jesus while the twelve Disciples were promoting him to the followers of John as the one whom God had sent to usher in the coming Kingdom? Simon/Peter has pointed our investigation along the proper path by articulating Matthias' was his constant companion from his baptism until his crucifixion.

Matthias, one may infer from the text quoted below, was with Jesus, accommodating him in his home, when John was executed.

Here is the evidence:

According to the Gospels, John was buried by his followers (Matthew 14:12; Mark 6:29), and only by the farthest stretch can one imagine his death went without a somber memorial gathering of his many devotees.

When news of John's execution reached Jesus, one may be confident the individual bearing that sad message also told him where the followers of John and his own Disciples were coming together to memorialize his passing.

Based on the text quoted above, Matthew 9:35 is the likely prefatory passage alerting us to an editorial redaction (alteration): "Then Jesus went about all the cities and villages...proclaiming the good news of the Kingdom, and curing every disease..." which is immediately followed by the historical, Matthias fragment: "When he (Jesus) saw the crowd he had compassion for them...because they were helpless, like sheep without a shepherd" (9:36).

Accompanied by Matthias to the southern side of the Sea of Galilee where John's followers had come together in a memorial gathering, Jesus, unaware he had been exalted by Simon/Peter and the other Disciples as God's Messiah, took a place to speak near the water's edge. The Disciples' fishing boat was wading-distance off-shore.

A "great crowd" suggests something special was happening. The description of sheep without a shepherd refers to the loss of a leader—namely John. Were there no other evidence, naturally one could assume the "shepherd" was Jesus speaking about himself, having been apart from the "gathered masses." But, in the Gospel of Mark, immediately following mention of John's burial (6:29-6:30) we read: "The Disciples gathered around Jesus and told him all that they had done and taught." They are plainly not the "sheep without a shepherd" to whom Jesus refers.

The DEFENSE asserts Matthias has preserved the record of Jesus saying, about John's followers, "They are like sheep without a shepherd." His account of the memorial gathering brings the episode to us for the first time: Matthias alone had the memory of Jesus' anguish and grief, and fully appreciated what Jesus meant when he replied to an exuberant Disciple, seeing him again for the first time since their separation following exclusion by the three lakeside villages (Mark 9:38) "Adon, we saw someone casting out demons in your name, and we tried to stop him..." But Jesus, apparently disheartened that he had been so widely rejected, replied (according to Luke 9:49) "whoever is not against you is for you."

Whereas the first three canonized Gospels, Matthew, Mark and Luke, are generally deemed a shared "synopsis" of Jesus' ministry with variations, John's Gospel is regarded as largely an evangelical blend of Jesus' earthly mission with his trans-mundane messianic promise. There are notable instances when John is also a synoptic resource. One such occasion is the Baptist's memorial gathering which the DEFENSE proffers, in John 6:1, is recognizably portraying the same episode from the following shared characteristics:

Matthew 14:14 "Jesus saw a great crowd..."

Mark 6:34   "...he saw a great crowd

JOHN 6:5   "...and he looked up and saw a large crowd..."

All three textual segments are associated with the famed miracle of Jesus providing bread to hungry bystanders: Matthew 14:19, Mark 6:44, Luke 9:15, and John: 6:11-14.

The significance for the DEFENSE is the continuing text, describing Jesus' reaction to the crowd in John 6:15:

"When Jesus realized the crowd was about to take him by force to make him King (of the Jews), he withdrew...."

Of such importance is this Matthias fragment, preserved by fortune and fate in the Gospel of John, the DEFENSE must pause to properly allocate its geographical setting on the lakeshore of the Sea of Galilee.

In deconstructing the narrative, we are faced with a mix of images in which the three major miracles–feeding masses from a small basket of bread and fish, walking on water, and calming the waves and wind of a storm on the water–occur in texts and passages suggesting a temporal proximity to the "great crowds without a shepherd." Of equal descriptive impact, in the same timeframe, is Jesus' supposed performance of large numbers of healings during that retreat to a "deserted place" to which people followed him, whereupon he fed and healed them...as they sat on the grass.

Who was in that crowd?

Not only John's followers and Jesus' Disciples, but spies for Herod Antipas. The DEFENSE shall prove they were not only present, but that Jesus recognized and addressed them, and was aware whatever he might say could be reported to the tetrarch.

Did it matter?

Jesus had never incited his listeners to rise up against the tetrarch. Only a call for the tetrarch's overthrow, or an invasion by an enemy king (such as John had possibly made) could lead to a charge of sedition and put him in danger. Unlike John he had not been guilty of such political incitement nor of condemning the tetrarch's marriage.

But he was filled with a solemn determination not to let John's murder silence him.

Despite the fragmentation, and whatever faith in the purported miracles a believing Christian has, the Gospel segment renders clarity to what has never before been recognized: Jesus gave a eulogy for his beloved cousin, John the Baptist, while on the grassy shore of the Sea of Galilee, away from the town limits from which he had been excluded. Here it is presented, with the DEFENSE especially focusing on Jesus' defiance of the punishment of John, that having been an execution carried out at the orders of Herod Antipas.

Jesus' eulogy for John

Luke 3:19-20 Matthew 14:12; Mark 6:29; Matthew 9:36; John 6:23; Matthew 9:38; Luke 9:49; Matthew 11:11-11:12; Luke 16:16; Matthew 11:18-19; Luke 7:33-34; Matthew 21:26; Matthew 16:24; Luke 11:29; Matthew 12:36; Mark 10:12; Matthew 19:9; Luke 18:11; John 6:15; Matthew 14:22; Mark 6:45

A summary of the content:

From Matthias' Gospel fragments, the DEFENSE proposes the following scenario approximates what actually occurred as Jesus commenced his homage to John.

Jesus began with his declaration to the crowd, "...the "Kingdom of Heaven has suffered violence and men of violence have taken it by force" (Matthew 11:12), a straightforward reprimand of the tetrarch,

35

Herodian administration members, and any complicit Pietists for their role in submissively contributing to or acquiescing in John's death.

His eulogy then expanded what would be textually preserved as Matthew 11:11: "Truly I say to you...there has never been anyone greater than John..."

(Note: I have deleted "born of woman..." because this is a phrase editorially inserted to make John seem an ordinary mortal when compared to Jesus, Christianized as the Son of God. Another phrase in the eulogistic soliloquy has Jesus say, "yet he who is least in the Kingdom is greater than he (John)." Oddly discordant with the sentiment of "none being greater than John," the words deserve brief scrutiny. First, they are like "born a woman," belittling John rather than lauding him. Of somewhat greater interest, is the wording, "least in the Kingdom," which recalls Jesus' statement about those who fail to keep the letter of Torah law being "the least in God's kingdom." The Matthew 5:17-5:19 passage is Christianized to mean Torah law would only be sacred until Jesus' mission (death and resurrection) were completed–so that abandoning Torah (being "least") would be the passport to high stature in the commencing Kingdom. Therefore the phrase "the least in the Kingdom will be greater than he" is Christologically inserted to mean "the one who dispenses with Torah will be greater than John." Luke 16:16 explicitly states that with John's death the Kingdom has begun–and Torah is replaced by preaching the Kingdom of God.

Significantly, when the phrase "born of woman..." and "least in the Kingdom is greater than he..." are deleted as enhancements, Jesus' praise of John shows that he did not consider himself superior to his cousin at all.

As Jesus continued his remarks, he took notice of the adversaries who were present.

"John came to you neither eating nor drinking and you say he was possessed. I eat and drink and you say, 'Behold, a glutton and drunkard, a friend of tax collectors and sinners...'" (Matthew 11:18-19; Luke 7:33-34).

Jesus then said: "When you went out into the wilderness (that is, to investigate John) what did you expect to see? A reed shaken by the wind? To see a man clothed in soft garments? Listen, those who wear plush clothing live in palaces."

It was an unmistakable castigation both of Antipas and of the Pietists who played an official role as members of the tetrarch's municipal council. Directing his remarks at them, the so-called "Herodians," Jesus decried their investigation of John. As the tetrarch's sycophants, they were nothing more than "reeds shaken in the wind," bending their beliefs to placate Antipas. Therefore, Jesus asked whether they had expected John to be like them, a reed who would bend in the political wind to maintain a position of authority. Unlike the Herodians, who were ruled by a man wearing plush clothes and living in a palace, John was concerned with God's Kingdom—and he was ruled not by men but by God.

Jesus was, with these words, delineating John's activity from the political realm—arguing that because his purpose was to prepare people for God's Kingdom, his intention could not have been treasonous.

To emphasize his point, he said: "I will ask you a question... the immersion by John, was it authorized by God or by men?" (Matthew 21:26)

When one of his Pietist adversaries then challenged him, "With what authority are you acting like this..." (Matthew 21:26) implying he should prove he had authority from God and show a sign from Heaven, he replied, "Why does this generation seek a sign? Truly I say to you no sign shall be given..." adding, "When it is evening you say it will be fair weather for the sky is red...you know how to interpret the appearance of the sky, but you cannot interpret the signs of the times. An evil and adulterous generation asks for a sign..."

In Matthew 16:24 and Luke 11:29 Jesus purportedly adds: "No sign shall be given except the sign of Jonah." Although these words are transparent enhancements intended to theologize Jesus' death as a sign to the Christian faithful, juxtaposing his three days in the tomb with Jonah's three days in the belly of the giant fish, it does have value as a textual link to Matthew 12:36. There, the "sign of Jonah" is preceded by words which may consequently be identified as part of the eulogy: "I tell you on the day of judgment (traditionally preceding the Kingdom of God), men will have to account for every careless word they utter. For by your words you will be (enabled to enter the Kingdom), and by your words (that is, bearing false witness against John) you will be condemned."

About then, having again vilified the Pietists as adulterers (Matthew 11:12), Jesus knew what they were all waiting to hear. Would he, like John, label the tetrarch's wife an adulteress? Jesus well understood the danger of the moment. *Were he to insult Herodias as John did, he too would become an enemy of the tetrarch. Putting himself at risk–though not for a capital offense of sedition as had John by implying support for the invasion by Aretas–Jesus' next words were courageous and fateful. "And if a woman divorces her husband," he declared, "and then marries another, she commits adultery" (Mark 10:12).*

Should one wonder whether Mark's text is anomalous, in that it stands alone as a version of Jesus' words, Paul's reiteration in I

Corinthians 7:10 specifically attributing the exact stricture to Jesus himself, confirms its authenticity.

Properly understood, Jesus had intended his incendiary remarks to give voice to his beloved cousin, John the Baptist, silenced for expressing his outrage at the defamation of Torah law manifest in the adulterous union called a marriage. Upon rendering his condemnation of the Pietists who turned their backs on John, and even may have (although this is uncertain) testified he had incited seditious support against the tetrarch, Jesus made an effort to depart.

According to the Gospel text, he dismissed the crowd and turned toward the offshore boat to leave for the other side of the lake.

Vividly, the Gospel of Matthew (8:18) preserves Matthias' record. His attempt to depart was impeded. The text states: "Now when Jesus saw great crowds around him, he gave orders to go over to the other side."

The next line reads: "A scribe...said, I'll accompany you." One may conjecture this is a scarce reference to Matthias.

What then happened, as portrayed in the Gospel of John 6:15, based on the temporal proximity to Jesus' departure from the crowd on the shore of the Sea of Galilee, was the dramatic episode of truly historic proportions:

"Jesus saw they intended to take him by force to be their king..."

...and he entered the water, trying to make his way to the Disciples' boat not far from shore (a surmise based on the succeeding Gospel text, Matthew 14:22 and Mark 6:45)–even as the assembled crowd heralded him "King"–surrounding and impeding his effort to wade to the boat, joining in an immersion that to many replicated John's baptisms, which, as the Gospel of John (6:15) suggests: They physically surrounded him, virtually forcing him to break free and escape their adoring grasp, "And he managed to get away." (The latter analytic of John 6:15 is based on the precipitous clarity it provides to the formerly opaque fragment in which Jesus appears so frenzied at the crowd's heralding him their King. Reassembled with the other eulogy fragments, the circumstances surrounding Jesus' sudden exposure to danger now follow.)

Despite his desperate effort to prevent their popular anointing of him as their "King of the Jews," they believed Jesus was the fulfillment of John's prophesy, anticipating a "King" to usher in God's Kingdom. Their faith this was so had been the result of Simon/Peter and the Disciples preaching their "good news" to John's followers during the period of John's incarceration, that same interval when Jesus had sent them away after he was denied entry into the precincts of Chorazin, Beit Zaida and Kfar Nahum.

[As stated earlier, the Gospel description of the Disciples influencing John's followers to have faith in Jesus as God's anointed Messiah while the Baptist was incarcerated, was unknown to Jesus. He had sent them off to spread the message of the Kingdom, after being banished by the three lakeside towns. Here again, is the cited text (Luke 7:22): "The blind see, the lame walk, lepers are cleansed, the deaf hear...Happy is the one who has faith in Jesus."]

Jesus also knew no dire threat loomed as he delivered the eulogy. Even though John was executed by Antipas for the seditious act of inciting popular rebellion on the side of the Nabataean warrior, Aretas —Jesus never crossed that line, nor would. He had implied only that the marriage between Herodias and the tetrarch was adulterous (Mark 10:12, during the eulogy).

So, as furious as Antipas might have been...as vengeful as he might have felt toward Jesus for echoing the insult to his marriage mouthed by John, there would be no basis for similar judicial reprisal under

Rome's system of jurisprudence until the unexpected "anointing" episode at his eulogy for John erupted.

The gathering of mourners evangelized by Simon/Peter thronged down the spring-breeze burnished–green grass bank of the Sea of Galilee, grabbed at his tunic, nearly preventing him from wading to the Disciples' fishing boat, and chanted: "King of the Jews! King of the Jews!" (as the Gospel of John 6:15 indicates). Their "coronation" threatened Jesus with a charge of inciting the crowd to rebellion, a capital crime of sedition, facing him with a corporeal threat for the first time.

[Note: In our determination to broaden the basis for considering Antipas a primary suspect, we must set aside his Gospel description that Antipas was "an open-minded man," who, prior to John's execution, had refused to acquiesce to Herodias' demand and kill him, because, "...he (John) was a righteous and holy man, and he protected him...and he liked to listen to him" (selectively, Mark 6:19-20). Eventually, as the Gospels record in grim detail, John was beheaded on Antipas' birthday only to satisfy his wife's request. (Another Gospel version suggests he was afraid of executing John because he was holy.)]

After the eulogy for John, when Jesus and the Disciples departed for "the other side" of the lake (Mark 6:45 linking to Matthew 16:5; Matthew 14:22; Mark 8:13), Antipas received reports about Jesus' eulogy and "coronation" as "King of the Jews" from "Pharisees" (Herodian-Pietists), those surveilling that grieving crowd.

Jesus' presentiment that reports of the crowd hailing him King of the Jews would reach the tetrarch, told his Disciples, "Beware the yeast of the Pharisees and the yeast of Herod" (Mark 8:15).

The "yeast" presumably was the corrupted truth, lies and distortions such as Jesus believed had been turned against John after the Baptist denounced the tetrarch's marriage. Only one thing protected Jesus from suffering the fate of John at the hands of Herod Antipas. There had been no grounds to charge him with sedition. All he had done was cite Torah law concerning adultery which applied to the tetrarch's Torah-taboo marriage. That was not a crime against the Empire, no matter how it angered Antipas. Still, the large crowd hailing him their anointed King of the Jews gave Jesus cause for serious concern for the first time.

The tetrarch's outraged response –a significant fragment of Matthias' Gospel text– upon his learning about Jesus at the lakeshore (which may have come as a message from Joanna, the wife of Chuza, who was a custodian in the Tiberius palace)– tells us much about his character:

> "John I beheaded. But who is this about whom I hear such things? (Luke 9:9) and, 'Is this John the Baptist raised from the dead?'" (Matthew 14:1-2), but most plainly rich in bitter sarcasm (Mark 6:16): "John whom I beheaded has been raised (from the dead)?"

If heretofore church doctrine has considered the above musings by Antipas to be expressions of spiritual "wonderment" over the seeming miracle of John's transmutation into the resurrected body of Jesus, we may virtually dismiss such a frivolous notion as more than stupefyingly ludicrous. The DEFENSE deems the effort by the authors of the canon to color Antipas' response with religious awe as an intentional diversion from his connection to the crucifixion, which we shall shortly detail.

Of central relevance is the fact that Herod Antipas heard of Jesus' eulogy, and the incriminating concomitant words and crowd-adoration soon after it occurred (Matthew 14:1-2; Mark 6:14-16; Luke

9:7-9) and was outraged to think another individual had "arisen" to replace John, in like manner insulting his wife as an adulteress, while being hailed as the Jewish "King," to usher in God's Kingdom.

If any doubt exists that Herod Antipas looked upon Jesus as "another John," that is resolved in Luke 13:31-33. This critical text supports the intention of Herod Antipas to do to Jesus what he had done to his cousin, the Baptist. Motivated by the insult to his marriage and based on a charge of sedition legitimized by Jesus supposedly inciting the crowd/masses to believe in him as "King of the Jews," a state-sanctioned manhunt was commenced.

We submit the following as central evidentiary text: (Luke 13:31-32) The passage reads: (Syntactically reconstructed to preserve the Matthias' fragment):

> "At that very hour some Pharisees came and said to him (Jesus), get away from here, for Herod (Antipas) wants to kill you."

> "He (Jesus) said to them, 'Go tell that fox for me...I (will) be on my way...(to Jerusalem).'"

Nothing essential to acquitting Antipas has been redacted from the above text. The words leave no doubt Antipas was determined to arrest Jesus and ultimately have him put to death.

Remarkably, those individuals who rush to alert Jesus warning him that his life was in danger were "Pharisees," the Jews of the Galilee constantly depicted as his adversaries and enemies, always challenging his role as rabbi and supposedly plotting his death. Their overhearing the ominous threat by Antipas, or learning of it so soon after he made it, indicates they were likely Herodians, Pietists in administrative positions, who were (based on the apparent Matthias fragment) determined to intercede and prevent another such atrocity as had been done to John.

Pertinent to the alleged motive of Jews wanting to kill Jesus for his pretense to being an authority over Torah law, one may keep in mind, John and Jesus were true to the commandment requiring a husband grant a wife full security through a divorce proceeding. Otherwise, a ruthless husband might force a woman to abandon her home with nothing, while he could say she had voluntarily left him, and find another woman to call his wife. Both John and Jesus had become enemies of Antipas for their criticism of the tetrarch's breach of the Torah's marital commandments.

If Pharisee Pietists/Herodians were urgently seeking to save Jesus, one has, even at this early juncture in the investigation, found cause to re-open the Gospel "case" blaming the Jews for participating in Jesus' murder on the cross.

Thus far the DEFENSE has identified Herod Antipas as a viable non-Hebrew suspect: He had the means (with authority as tetrarch of the Galilee) to orchestrate a state-sanctioned arrest and judicial proceeding, a motive (the insult to his marriage and especially, Herodias), a basis for arrest on a capital charge of sedition (Jesus having been ceremonially anointed "King of the Jews" at the eulogy for his cousin, John the Baptist), and had made a threat to kill Jesus, which led to Jesus' reply: "tell that fox I am leaving his region…"

Did Jesus ever wonder where John's followers got the idea he was "King of the Jews?"

If the DEFENSE argument is correct, and the Disciples evangelized John's followers with the belief in Jesus as God's Son, while they had been sent off on their own and he was banished from the three towns, he would have been unaware of their exalting him

44

as having Divine origins. As observed above, when he met up with them again, at the eulogy, they excitedly began to inform him of their activities in his absence (Mark 9:38; Luke 9:49). Therefore, he would have been stunned by John's grieving followers anointing him, "King of the Jews," as he waded to the Disciples' fishing boat forcing himself free from their grasp.

Did Jesus have a reaction to their heralding him King of the Jews? He almost certainly would have been determined to find out just who had been fostering the basis for a charge of sedition.

The famed passage in Luke 9:18-20 when their boat, after a stop in Magdala, continued to the far side of the Sea of Galilee, reaching the shore of Caesaria Philippi, quotes Jesus as confronting Simon/Peter: "Who do the crowds say I am...who do you say I am?" he demanded.

Simon/Peter answered: "The Messiah" (Literally: "Anointed one of God," or, "King of the Jews"), the one to rule the coming Kingdom.

Jesus was furious. "You and the (others) must not say such things about me," he rebuked. "...because I will be...killed..." (Matthew 16:21; Mark 8:31; 9:22)...to which Simon/Peter responded (Matthew 16:22): "This will never happen to you..." a phrase omitted from the other gospels.

The text which arguably has been interpreted to fit the mold of church kerygmata, sanctifying Jesus' intent to be crucified in Jerusalem reads: (Jesus castigating Simon/Peter, Mark 8:33)

> "You are setting your mind not on divine
> things, but on human things...
> "Get behind me satan!"

The "not Divine things" to which Jesus (per Matthias) refers was a misshapen perception he was King of the Jews. He tells Simon/

Peter, "You are setting your mind <u>not on divine things</u>–meaning Jesus himself–by failing to realize he was walking alongside a human being–meaning, Jesus was not a god, and therefore could be arrested and die.

Not only had Jesus called Simon/Peter "satan" for fostering a possible charge of sedition, but angrily adds (Mark 8:33) that Simon/Peter should literally stop walking near his side and get in back of him, plainly because he had heard enough of his mischaracterization.

A Matthias fragment adds: (Matthew 7:21-7:23; Luke 13:26 reassembled): "Why are you always calling me 'Lord' when I tell you not to. No one who calls me 'Lord' will enter the Kingdom of God...many will say to me 'Lord, Lord, did we not prophesy and cast out demons in your name...' and I will declare to them 'I never knew you.'" Luke adds a vivid comment: "You will say we ate and drank with you, and you taught in our company...but I will say I don't know where you come from..."

Here, the DEFENSE must recognize the extraordinary spiritual test Simon/Peter faced at this very juncture. The canonized Gospel text illuminates Simon/Peter's deeply tortured soul upon Jesus' retreat following the eulogy for John. Far more than his part in having made Jesus a target of Herod Antipas, his role in abetting Jesus' arrest and possible crucifixion was unimaginable.

(Matthew 16:22): "This will never happen to you..." he insists, obviously incapable of conceiving such a calamity.

Jesus the man was, after all, his Christ, the savior and Son of God. He could not even be arrested, much less die; little wonder, then, Simon/Peter asserted his post-crucifixion editorial authority to align Gospel text with the new theology's salvation agenda.

Caesaria Philippi textual reprimands were altered to become a coded reference to the hour when Jesus was intending to reveal himself in Jerusalem. Simon/Peter was called "satan" because he had prematurely put God's plan at risk by telling people who Jesus was before the time was right for his Divine identity to become known.

Matthias' written record containing his (proto)fragment: "Jesus said to Simon/Peter, 'You are walking at the side of a man, not a god...' became, with poetic enhancement, Simon/Peter's mind was on earthly things, not God's plan for the Kingdom.

When Jesus told him to stop calling him, "Lord," that was because his identity was to be kept a secret...

When Jesus said to him he would be arrested and killed...that had to be God's plan yet to unfold in Jerusalem, where after three days he would rise again.

Contrary to the clarity Matthias' testimony provides, fully portraying Jesus as a fugitive from "that fox" (Herod Antipas), Jesus' Divine armor of miraculous powers, embellishments with which Simon/Peter adorns his Gospel image, prevents any mortal danger threatening to disrupt the Jerusalem crucifixion/resurrection schedule.

IV

The Defense of the Jews

[A Procedural note: The DEFENSE has established Herod Antipas' motive and expressed intent to kill Jesus. His opportunity and direct role in causing Jesus' crucifixion shall be presented following the analysis of Jesus' interrogation by the High Priest, Caiaphas. The DEFENSE is aware that while our evidence satisfies every requirement to prove beyond any doubt Herod Antipas had motive and had made the indicated threat, our proof he was guilty of the crime remains an unlitigated issue in this treatise. We shall first address the doctrinal guilt of the Jews, which is step-by-step to be rejected in totality.]

Following his arrest, Jesus was led to Caiaphas' house for the interrogation, and Matthias was permitted entry as an episkopas (administrative supervisor of note) acquainted with the High Priest, while Simon/Peter was required to wait outside (John 18:15-16).

Inside Caiaphas' house, Matthias' fragmented record, assembled from the midst of confabulated textual enhancement, preserves the true Gospel account.

The DEFENSE proceeds to fully present the supposed testimony including any given by "the Council, elders, chief priests, scribes, or crowds" (far more likely only a sparse handful of Herodians from

Antipas' retinue for the planned purpose of securing a preordained outcome) that Jesus claimed to be "King of the Jews." Were there no such testimony by two eyewitnesses, no finding of guilt would be made.

The hearing before Caiaphas

The array of presumed witnesses and charges against Jesus are different in each Gospel. In his appearance before Caiaphas, the Gospel of John says only that he was "asked questions about his teaching." When he again indicated (as in Mark 14:49 at the scene of his arrest) that the guards have heard him in the Temple–and know he did or said nothing wrong–one of them slapped him in the face.

In the Gospels of Matthew and Mark witnesses came forward to charge Jesus with threatening violence to the Temple, one saying he boasted he could destroy it and the other, he would destroy it, probably not a crime, as unlikely as it is that he ever said such a thing about God's House, and certainly not a transgression punishable by death. And, in both their testimony these "witnesses" quote his supposed claim to have power to rebuild it in three days. (The three-day time frame is a repetitive Christianizing component evoking his resurrection after three days in the tomb.) Neither Luke nor John make reference to such testimony. Notably, Mark 14:56 states: "Many bore false witness against him and their testimony did not agree." The Gospel of Matthew (26:60) says much the same thing. In all four Gospels, however, only one charge is paramount, the one which will ultimately be a capital crime of sedition under Roman law, as we know from the inscription over the cross, citing his claim to be King of the Jews ("Jesus of Nazareth King of the Jews"). Contrary to the image of venomous Jews generated by embedded church doctrine, none among the Jewish witnesses testified he was guilty of claiming to be King of the Jews.

At the hearing before Caiaphas, Jesus was asked to say whether he was or was not the Messiah-king. (The word "Christ" in Matthew, Mark and Luke migrates from the Greek and Latin vernacular, but would not have been used by the High Priest or traditional Jews.) In Matthew 26:64 the text reads: "(Caiaphas demanded)...tell us if you are the (Messiah-king), the Son of God," to which Jesus replied, "You have said it..." This formulation was a legal counter-accusation that the accuser was bearing false witness.

What was the falsehood? No other possibility exists as to what he meant. They were falsely accusing him of claiming to be King of the Jews.

Because his usage is in the day's legal vernacular, the question persists as to whether he actually denied being the Messiah. Put simply: Why didn't Jesus tell his accusers, "I do not claim to be, nor am I the anointed Son of God. I never pretended to be the King of the Jews sent to usher in and rule God's Kingdom on earth"?

The legal formulation, accusing the accuser of bearing false witness, was actually Jesus' only recourse, since, no matter what denial he made that he believed himself King, he would still have been considered guilty of fraudulently misrepresenting himself as King and so, seditiously misleading the Jewish populace (Luke 23:4).

Whether, in fact, he was a religious fraud–stirring up the masses by falsely claiming to be King of the Jews–or actually believed it about himself, made no legal difference, if eyewitnesses came forward to testify against him. Either way, he was guilty of sedition–a verdict that he could not change by testifying in his own behalf.

When Caiaphas demanded, "Tell us if you are the Messiah-king," Jesus replied: "If I tell you, you will not believe" (a meaning Matthias' text more properly implies: "No matter what I say, you will think I am guilty. If I tell you I am not King of the Jews–nor have I ever claimed to be–you will not believe me." (Precipitous from Matthias: "If I say this to you, you will not believe, and if I question you, you will not answer" Luke 22:67-68. Note: "Precipitous" refers to the critical method of achieving luminous insight by conjoining formerly obscure syntactical fragments. See Forward for further elucidation.)

Reworded by the Gospel author of Mark 14:61-62, the revised text has Jesus affirm his Divine identity, saying, "I am (King of the Jews)." This rather astounding self-revelation, in that it stands alone at the hearing as such, is actually a severed fragment of Luke 22:70. That text, in full, as it occurs in the Lukan version is Jesus' supposed reply to "all of the (Jewish Temple Council)" when asked, "'Are you the Son of God?' he said to them, 'You say that I am'" (Mark 14:62). Adroitly deleted are the words,"You say that..." leaving the proclamation of his Divinity, "I am." Because the words "I am" were actually spoken by Jesus, the editorial revision, though a fabricated meaning, would not have been regarded as falsifying Matthias' record of Jesus' direct testimony.

What role did Jews play in Jesus' hearing before Caiaphas?

In attempting to credibly address this question, the DEFENSE must first filter the Gospel voice which has led to millennia of fulminating Christian hatred, separating the possible involvement of Jews from the impossible. Keeping in mind, none of Jesus' Disciples– excepting (as we argue) Matthias–were witnesses, the varied Gospel entries, as different as they are one from the other, were altered from Matthias' original account. Still, searching for their shared theme, and his likely record of events, one is struck by the fact they have this in common: At least some of the (most likely, Herodian Pietist) Jews at the hearing before Caiaphas were called to give testimony.

According to Jewish law, a death sentence required at least two eyewitnesses. Therefore, those claiming to have seen Jesus "stir up the People" (Luke 23:5) seditiously acting like a God-sent King, were legally necessary for the indictment on a charge of sedition.

Given Torah law was strictly enforced in a capital proceeding, one may assume two would have to testify, "I saw and heard him claim to be King of the Jews."

Selectively, here is how the Gospels describe the problem in getting the Jewish witnesses to provide testimony supporting a guilty verdict: "Now (Caiaphas) sought testimony against Jesus necessary to put him to death, *but could get none* (my italics)–and their testimony did not agree" (Matthew 26:59-60; Mark 14:55-56).

Caiaphas, paying little heed to what else the witnesses said, since it did not matter, tried to get Jesus to confess to the actual charge: "Tell us if you are the Messiah/King of the Jews!" (Here, returning the word "Christ" to its equivalent Jewish vernacular) (Mark 14:61; Luke 22:67).

Despite the High Priest's determination to obey Torah law regarding witnesses, he failed. Frustrated, he declared, telling those who apparently demurred, "It is better that only he die–than many with him" (John 18:14).

To conclude: The High Priest formally demanded Jesus testify whether he was King of the Jews (the Messiah) or not. (Matthew 26:63) The "Council," elders, chief priests and scribes (Luke 22:67) likewise are described as interrogating him: "If you are the King of the Jews (the Messiah) tell us."

The Gospels agree: Jesus replied to all in similar wording, "You are the ones who say so," or, "you are accusing me of saying it." If the accusation was baseless, those making it were violating the Torah's commandment against taking Adonai's name in vain and bearing false witness. According to Torah, the punishment was to be the same as that which was directed against the individual falsely accused.

Although uncertainty remains whether Caiaphas, the High Priest, believed Jesus considered himself King of the Jews, given there is no evidence to instruct us as to his opinion, he plainly was astonished no witnesses said they ever heard Jesus breathe a word suggesting he was.

As the DEFENSE shall now argue, Antipas had made his intentions clear to the High Priest that he was in league with Pontius Pilate to assure the crucifixion of Jesus. It either was going to happen, or there would be blood flowing across the Temple courts. (The evidence for the agreement between Pilate and Antipas shall be produced below.)

Frustrated by his failure to have any of the supposed "bloodthirsty" Jews testify, Caiaphas demanded: "Why do we still need witnesses!" (Matthew 26:65; Mark 14:63) whereupon the High Priest made the remark "It is better for one man to die for many, than for many to die for one," and, as the Gospel of John 18:28 reports: "Then they took Jesus from Caiaphas to Pilate's headquarters..."

The Gospel of Luke suggests that after reaching Pontius Pilate, the witnesses who never testified against Jesus hours earlier when they were with Caiaphas, now, in one single phrase, did so for the first time, saying they heard him claim to be King of the Jews (Luke 23:2). This is an obvious effort to supply testimony which did not exist. Its relocation to the Gabbatha scene of judgment before Pilate isolates it as a doctrinal artifact of no historic merit.

In sum:

The DEFENSE submits the foregoing analysis has returned the Gospelic portrayal of the Caiaphas hearing to the Matthias original, which, unlike the canonized version, demonizing the Jews as lusting for Jesus' death on the cross, reveals those present were altogether resistant to his indictment.

The testimony of the single Disciple–so-described in the Gospels (identified as Matthias)– the one alone permitted entry to the interrogation in Caiaphas' house, states that NO WITNESS came forward to testify THEY EVER HEARD HIM CLAIM TO BE KING OF THE JEWS; not one, and not the two necessary to reach a verdict of "guilty." Each time Jesus was challenged to say whether he believed himself to be the "King of the Jews" his reply was a legalistic response threatening the inquirer with the counter-charge of bearing false witness, invoking the law, with the formulation: "They are your words."

[Note: Caiaphas' refusal to save Jesus may invite the response he was the High Priest and sent Jesus to his death...but, the DEFENSE shall show he had actually been threatened by Pontius Pilate that his failure to comply would result in a massacre of the local population under the pretext of rebellious uprisings.]

In its unabated display of verbal contempt for the Jews, the post-crucifixion Gospel text supplements Matthias' depiction with passages describing a "Council of Jews" augmented by so-called, "chief priests, elders, and scribes," who participated in handing over Jesus to Pilate, agreeing he deserved death and therefore, as the drama unfolded, were soon after represented demanding of Pontius Pilate, "Crucify him!" None, or certainly very few, stop to ask, why if the gathered witnesses in the Caiaphas' hearing were so determined to see Jesus die on the cross, did they not simply say, "We heard him claim to be King of the Jews"? To suggest they held back out of reluctance to bear false witness, is to agree they saw no legal reason for him to be put to death. One may, with certainty, conclude, they were unwilling to encourage the killing on the cross of an innocent man.

The DEFENSE shall formally disprove the Gospel portrayal of bloodthirsty Jewish leaders gathered or convened with Temple administrators for the extra-judicial judgment of Jesus, such as it was, to decree and demand a death sentence for a crime with no witnessed testimony, for a seditious claim to be king, which none said they ever heard him make.

First, our case turns to the documentation of Herod Antipas' guilt in orchestrating and bringing to grim fruition his murder of Jesus.

Directly after the hearing and interrogation in Caiaphas' house, Jesus was brought before Pontius Pilate for judgment and sentencing.

Much has been made of Pilate's benign response to the specified complaints of the Jews, which he appears to believe hardly rose to the level of a serious criminal infraction, certainly not warranting crucifixion. The DEFENSE is interested, at this juncture not in the clamor for punishment by the supposed, gathered Jewish leaders represented textually as noisily making their contempt for Jesus known, but in the appearance of none other than Herod Antipas.

According to Luke 23:6-12, upon learning that Jesus was a Galilean, and "was under Herod Antipas' jurisdiction, he (Pilate) sent him off to Herod Antipas who was himself in Jerusalem at the time."

Here, the DEFENSE enters into the record that Pontius Pilate officially authorized Herod Antipas as the individual to be administratively responsible for the fate of Jesus and the outcome of the judicial proceeding underway (Luke 23:6-7).

As if Antipas had no primary agenda to kill Jesus, the Gospel text offers an image of an ambivalent tetrarch. When Jesus is brought before him, we are initially presented with the canonized description of this as his disposition:

"When Herod saw Jesus he was very glad. For he had been wanting to see him for a long time, for he had heard about him and was hoping to see him perform some sign..."

This Lukan passage fails the test of historical value on its face. "Wanting to see him for a long time..." makes it sound like the eulogy for John the Baptist was many months, or perhaps a year earlier– when, in actuality, Jesus indirectly called Herodias an adulteress, echoing his cousin's fatal harangue, only weeks earlier. That was when Antipas made his threat to kill Jesus, leading those Herodian Pharisees, contrary to our image of ghoulish, vindictive Jews, to warn, "Herod wants to kill you!"

Could Herod Antipas have been "Glad to see Jesus"? We need not wonder how far from the truth this statement strays, when we recognize the next description of Antipas' role places him in the midst of "The chief priests and scribes (who) stood by vehemently accusing (Jesus)..." (23:10)

If Herod Antipas just happened to be in Jerusalem, so that Pontius Pilate sent Jesus off to be interrogated and judged by him under Galilean authority, where did those chief priests and scribes suddenly come from? Did they just happen to be there with Antipas too?

Adding to this canonical record so replete with attempts to show Jewish complicity (the accusing elders, priests and scribes), Herod Antipas, at first "glad to see Jesus," is suddenly, and discordantly, turned into his hateful antagonist, filled with loathing.

Luke 23:11 reads: "Even Herod Antipas and his soldiers treated him (Jesus) with contempt and mocked him. They put an elegant robe on him and sent him back to Pilate."

The disdain Antipas vented toward Jesus is preserved in Matthias' textual record. His venomous feelings towards Jesus, exhibited in the acts mocking him as a would-be king stand as precipitously clear evidence of Antipas' guilt when reassembled as we have done in this segment of the treatise.

Despite the passage opening with Herod Antipas supposedly situated somewhere in Jerusalem, other than in the presence of Pontius Pilate, two criteria establish he was observing the proceeding just behind the "Gabbatha" stone-paved court of judgment, likely in the building doorway of the so-called "Praetorium" headquarters.

The royal purple robe (Luke 23:11, euphemistically worded as "elegant" or "bright") is first put on Jesus to mock him as a "would-be" King of the Jews NOT by Pontius Pilate's cohort, but by the soldiers of Herod Antipas.

John 19:2-4 switches the protagonist role to Pilate, replacing Antipas.

After dressing Jesus in the royal robe of mockery (as if the one placed on Jesus by Antipas never happened) Pilate states, "I am bringing him out to you to let you know that I find no case against him..."

Reconstructed from the Matthias fragments, the one emerging from the Praetorium courtyard with Jesus dressed in the robe of mockery and wearing a crown of thorns (John 19:5) was Herod Antipas, not Pontius Pilate. This is a significant indication the tetrarch was fully cognizant of the charge of sedition facing Jesus, the basis for the sentence of crucifixion to avenge the insult to Herodias. He did not need to be told to mock him as King of the Jews because he was the one bringing the accusation Jesus had been anointed God's chosen ruler at the eulogy for John.

Of critical importance in concluding Herod Antipas was, beyond doubt, the perpetrator of Jesus' state-orchestrated murder, that he was its instigator and ultimate adjudicator, is the final seal on the case file: the dramatized mockery by Antipas' cohort, forcing Jesus to dress as a caricature king for having allegedly claimed to be King of the Jews–a crime of sedition which no Jews testified they had ever witnessed, and one to which Jesus never confessed. The DEFENSE has earlier traced back the fabricated charge to Simon/Peter's evangelical activity indoctrinating the followers of John to revere Jesus as "King of the Jews" which became an anointing ceremony contra Jesus' will– at the memorial gathering for John.

The DEFENSE now intends to support with evidence the actual reason Caiaphas was forced by Pontius Pilate, in league with Herod Antipas (*at the latter's discretion, since Jesus was a Galilean)*, to surrender Jesus for judgment knowing he would be crucified.

According to Josephus, whose writing was nearly contemporaneous with these events, for years, Antipas and Pontius Pilate had no love for one another. Stemming from a case taken before the emperor Tiberius for a decision some years earlier, they held each other in contempt. On that occasion, Antipas had protested Pilate's issuing coins with idolatrous imagery (the littus and simpulum), as well as permitting Roman soldiers to enter Jerusalem with armor bearing the emperor's image. Apparently acting in behalf of his loyal Herodian Pietists, the tetrarch succeeded in persuading Tiberius to overrule Pilate, who was forced to stop circulating the coins or adorning the military with their graven images (Josephus; Antiquities 18:3, 56-57).

More recently, however, Pilate was again faced with a potential popular uprising, this time from Samaritans, not Jews. Though matters were not yet out of hand, the Syrian Legate Vitellius was certainly prepared to force Pilate to present himself before Tiberius and defend any too-harsh subjugation of that Samaritan community which he was known to despise.

Politically, Herod Antipas was far more valuable to Pontius Pilate as an ally than as a foe. Any misstep or perceived popular unrest the governor/procurator of Jerusalem might cause which was appealed to Vitellius, the Roman legate under whose supervision and constraint he administered Jerusalem, if brought before Emperor Tiberius, could result in his ouster. To have Antipas weigh in on his behalf, testifying his actions, whatever they might be, were warranted, would be politically invaluable.

Poised as Nabataea's camel brigades were on the border of Antipas' tetrarchy, he and Pilate's most recent mutual concern for stability in the region was well-known, as an incursion by Aretas IV appeared an ever-more possible eventuality (to avenge the marriage to Herodias which humiliated his own Arab daughter).

Although Antipas certainly had harbored ill-will toward Pontius Pilate for threatening his loyal Herodians with death for their protests over the emperor's ritual icons on coins and shields, he was apparently prepared to let bygones be bygones in exchange for the life of Jesus, evidenced in the text wherein Pilate delegates to the tetrarch the administrative authority for a judicial verdict deciding Jesus' fate as a Galilean resident (Luke 23:6-7).

Once Herod Antipas had brought the charge of sedition, formally accusing Jesus of claiming to be "King of the Jews," the Roman law satisfying the conditions for a death sentence on the cross had been met.

[Note: An excerpt from the Jewish Encyclopedia (Crucifixion: by Kaufmann Kohler, G. Hirsch) states:

"Many of the Jews suspected of Messianic ambitions had been nailed to the cross by Rome. The Messiah, "king of the Jews," was a rebel in the estimation of Rome, and rebels were crucified (Suetonius, "Vespas." 4; "Claudius," xxv.; Josephus, "Ant." xx. 5, § 1; 8, § 6; Acts v. 36, 37). The inscription on the cross of Jesus reveals the crime for which, according to Roman law, Jesus expired. He was a rebel. Tacitus ("Annales," 54, 59) reports therefore without comment the fact that Jesus was crucified. For Romans no amplification was necessary."]

So it was, that sharing a laugh at the sight of the foolish-looking king, "Antipas and Pilate became friends with each other...for before this they had been enemies" (Luke 23:12).

V

The Motive for Scapegoating the Jews

In the prior section, the verdict of this treatise is clear and decisive: Herod Antipas, having motive and opportunity, participated in the judicial proceeding which by pre-arranged, mutual agreement between himself and Pontius Pilate culminated in what may truly be described as history's most consequential and tragic injustice ever done to a single individual.

The Jews, never having testified Jesus committed the crime of sedition with which he was charged and crucified, acting contrary to the demands of the Jewish High Priest in their unwillingness to provide condemning testimony, are, with this finding, fully acquitted of any responsibility for Jesus' arrest, the outcome of his hearing, the judgment orchestrated by Herod Antipas, and the consequent sentence of crucifixion for sedition as "King of the Jews." Any blame attaching to the High Priest as an administrative functionary of the Roman overlords, revealing his subordinate status by stating to the reticent gathering of Jews, "It is better one man die than many," expressed his forced submission to the rule of the governing authority, and made it plain that he was acting against his own will.

Still unanswered are two central questions:

A. Did "establishment" Jews ever hope or plot to kill Jesus? and,

B. Why did Simon/Peter turn on the Jews (in his presumed role as originator and overseer of the earliest Gospel testament), with such unrestrained malice, accusing them in so many passages of intentionally fostering circumstances leading to Jesus' death, the very thing which his own evangelizing had caused, just as Jesus warned him it would?

A. Did "establishment" Jews ever hope or plot to kill Jesus?

Vilified in repeated textual tropes, the Jews are inalterably the target of the Gospels' venomous narrative, of which numerous examples may be found in the earlier section (II: "A General Accusation").

In the following segment, the DEFENSE shall make this assertion: the derogation of the Jews as would-be killers of a man they may, or may not, have perceived to be a misguided teacher imparting false Torah doctrine, even if he breached such rabbinic customs as the stricture against healing on Shabbat, would not and did not lead to his pursuit by Herod Antipas, or hearing before Caiaphas, much less his execution for transgressions which he himself argued did not violate Torah law (Mark 3:4 and others).

To wit, the DEFENSE has already introduced evidence that Pharisees warned Jesus about Herod Antipas' intention to kill him. Further, at the Caiaphas hearing, witnessed by Matthias (conclusively shown above), all Jews refused to testify he had committed the crime for which he was crucified.

With these facts in mind, the DEFENSE now lists the chief motives <u>ascribed</u> to the Jews for wanting to kill Jesus.

1. Jesus **equated** himself with God.
2. The Jews were **jealous/envious** of him (for being God's Son and having the Divine authority to perform the miracles and wonders they witnessed.)
3. The Jews **rejected** Jesus as Christ, the "King of the Jews."

Let us consider the three possibilities:

First, to suggest they wanted to kill a rabbi who claimed to be imbued with spiritual guidance from our Creator, hardly rings true. After all, our sages relied upon the ruach ha-kodesh (the "holy spirit") in teaching Torah and performing healings much as did Jesus, and prayed in the same synagogues as he.

For the Gospels to ascribe to the Jews venom towards Jesus for **"equating"** himself with God does not match the facts. The DEFENSE has shown Jesus shunned such self-exaltation.

Notably, in John 10:34 Jesus quotes Psalm 82:6 to show what he means by saying he is a son of God, explaining to his critics that Jewish tradition speaks of those who are righteous as 'sons of God.' Further, Jesus on more than one occasion argued in rabbinic fashion his healings on Shabbat did not transgress the Torah, nor show his authority to supersede Torah law– for he knew there was no such Torah prohibition. That the Gospels suggest Pietist Jews watched to see if he would violate the Torah by healing on the Sabbath is to presume they were ignorant of Torah law, when, at most, they were aggravated he ignored their rabbinic customs when he considered them hypocritical or heartless. Among varied examples of his denials of a Divine identity, one should recall his remonstration directed to his Disciples, "Why do you call me good. Only God is good!" (Mark 10:18)

As for calling God his "father," a supposed heresy, Jews had always done that in their prayers.

Nor should we omit from the list, his rebuke of Simon/Peter for nurturing the rumor of his Divine origins: "You and the (others) must not say such things about me," he rebuked. "...because I will be... killed..." (Matthew 16:21; Mark 8:31; 9:22). Further documented, no Jewish witnesses ever testified against him that they ever heard him claim to be "King of the Jews."

[If one finds it hard to believe that Jews have borne the bizarre blame for killing a Divinity, when that is by definition impossible, the modern disputation over that very issue by the Vatican during its birth pangs of the Nostra Aetatis are illuminating. As Professor Susannah Heschel has detailed in a recent chapter, "Out of the Mystery Comes the Bond" (Essays in Honor of John T. Pawlikowski, OSM Mahwah, NJ: Paulist Press, 2018, 199-225) her renowned father, Abraham Joshua Heschel (z"l), blamed the charge of deicide against the Jews as a two-millennia cause of persecution and influenced Cardinal Bea to influence Vatican change of Catholic doctrine on that view. Importantly, Professor Heschel includes the following resulting observation concerning the Catholic church dialogue on the subject of Jewish deicide which her father had influenced: "Cardinal Bea... emphasized that the Jews could not be accused of deicide.... Cardinal Ruffini gave the main (Vatican council, 1964) speech: he agreed that deicide should be abandoned (asserting)—"no one can kill God."]

Nonetheless, as noted in Part I of this treatise, the final version of the Catholic formulary **_removed_** the following words: ***"The Jewish people never should be represented as*** rejected or accursed, or ***guilty*** *of deicide."* In other words, the Catholic church just could not let go of that traditional cornerstone of hate.

Let us consider the second possibility:

Surely, if the Jews believed he was their anointed King sent by God to usher in the prophesied Kingdom, how could they have been anything but overwhelmed with joy? Yet, the Gospels attribute the Jewish bloodlust to a satanic **"envy"** over Jesus' Divine authority and ability to work miracles.

The text of Mark 15:10 states "...it was out of jealousy that the chief priests had handed him over," conjuring Jews who were supposedly determined to kill the Son of God because his miracles were real, and, therefore so was his Divine identity.

Does this make sense?

In the age of Greek myths when those famed gods of Olympus such as Zeus, achieved glory by subduing lesser gods, the term "deicide" enjoyed a meaning contextualized in archaic drama. Today, its use is an oxymoron. How, after all can God be killed? The very definition of our Creator is His immortality. That, after all is the similar belief Jesus has eternal life, witnessed and borne out in spiritual communion by disciples, apostles and devotees.

But, the Catholic church and Vatican II, in their final version of their Nostra Aetate, could not bring themselves to acquit the Jews of pressing for deicide (whether out of satanic envy, or any other reason) although, according to Gospel theology, envious Jews who believed Jesus was the Christ surely would have known trying to kill him was pointless.

Of utmost significance, the Gospels' depict ghoulish Jews demanding Jesus' crucifixion, because the "Council, chief priests, elders, and scribes" **rejected** the Christian savior and were imbued by a murderous lust for his death to prove he was not the Christ.

The DEFENSE now proffers:

When Jesus berated Simon/Peter for calling him, "King of the Jews," because saying such things could lead to his death, he cried out to Jesus, "Lord, this cannot happen to you!" (Matthew 16:22) only to be answered (the Matthias reconstruction): "You don't realize you are walking at the side of a man, not a god..."

Without exaggeration, the words spoken by Jesus, preserved by Matthias, were the true rejection by Jesus himself of any notion he was the Christ. The DEFENSE asserts Jesus himself spoke these words in an attempt to stop Simon/Peter from believing in a god he had created to save him, but which, as Jesus foresaw, if publicly proclaimed to herald his rule as "King of the Jews," would put him on a path to execution.

[NOTE: The fact is those Herodian spies at John's eulogy were Jews and did play a role in agitating Antipas. But that hardly supports a more general argument "the Jews did have a role in Jesus' demise." One need only observe what Jesus has to say about them: (Mark 8:15) "Beware of the yeast (that is, lies) of the Pharisees and the yeast (lies) of Herod." The charge Jesus claimed to be "King of the Jews" would be a a falsehood, "yeast," if they ever said he said such a thing about himself. BUT DID THEY? Both during his escape, when he is warned by members of that very same group of Palace Pharisee-Herodians (Luke 13:31-32) (!) Herod wants to kill you, and at the Caiaphas' "hearing," when Pharisees and other Jews refuse to accuse him of claiming to be "King of the Jews," one is aware the few miscreants who may have succored Antipas' lust to avenge the perceived insult to his marriage by bringing a malicious report of the eulogy condemnation of his conjugal adultery were hardly more than a minuscule representation of the Jewish Galilean community, having motives which were self-edification, not Jesus' death.

Further, if some would suggest I have too readily dismissed the argument that based on Galilean Pietistic antipathy toward Jesus, such as was exhibited by the three towns banishing him, or the confrontational arguments recorded as a result of his provocative healings on Shabbat, and derisive criticism of Pietist hypocricy, there was sufficient motive to kill him, I reject that position as specious. Such harsh confrontations concerning approaches to Torah law among rabbis are attested in the Talmud, and even constitute the basis for establishing accepted ritual obligations and observance.]

Gospel texts illuminate the serious issue Simon/Peter was facing. After Jesus had been crucified, the horrific event threatened to destroy his world of faith. Jesus the man was, after all, his Christ, the savior and Son of God sent to be sacrificed for the sins of mankind. Therefore, he appended Matthias' testimony, altering his witnessed record revamping the actual wording, to read as follows:

"(I must undergo)...great suffering, and be <u>rejected</u> by the elders, the chief priests and the scribes and be killed and in three days rise again (Mark 8:31; Luke 9:22).

The conviction expressed in this DEFENSE, based on the evidence, is that Simon/Peter could not accept Jesus' own words, the words of the one he considered a Divinity, the Son of God. Denying the prima facie intent of Jesus' rebuke for his dangerous exaltations, he clung desperately to the false Jesus he had created to save him.

Therefore, Simon/Peter, who was unable to even comprehend the unimaginable notion Jesus could himself be the chiefmost "Christ-killer," perceived the recalcitrant Jews, those "rejectors" of their own anointed King, as destroyers of faith in his Divinity.

In a significant departure from what historical studies have generally observed, this treatise asserts that Jews who were aware of Jesus' short ministry and his final travail, acted towards him as if he was no different than they were, and whatever criticism they may have directed at him for breaking legal regulations stemming from rabbinic custom hardly led them to harbor seething contempt such as the Gospels describe.

Simon/Peter understood the implications of the Jewish rejection of Jesus as God's Son.

Because their widespread indifference,* a manifest negative influence, could threaten to kill faith in him as the Christ, Simon/Peter's fledgling theology appeared to be in desperate need of his doctrinal salvation.

*[How many Jews became Christians in the first century?

The failure of the Christian mission to the Jews, according to scholar David C. Sim, in his scrupulously researched paper (written as Hugo Gryn Fellow in Religious Tolerance at the Centre for Jewish/Christian Relations, Cambridge, 2003) was staggering. He states:

"...there is no evidence from either Christian or non- Christian sources that this church later made significant conversions among the population of Jerusalem. It remained from beginning to end a small and largely un-influential group within the city. Calculating the precise size of the Jerusalem church at any time is fraught with obvious danger, but I would argue that its numbers at no time exceeded 500. For much of its history, it may have been considerably smaller than this."

And, referring to the emerging faction of Jerusalem-centered Christians (which I propose was promulgated by Simon/Peter) who observed Torah law versus the Pauline faction in the north who abdicated most central dietary rituals and circumcision: "It is important to evaluate each of these Christian traditions in its own right and on its own terms, and to gauge the respective success or otherwise of each. It will be maintained...that neither of them, not even the Law- observant tradition, made much impact at all among the Jews of the first century."]

To prevent the looming calamity, Simon/Peter, collaborated with those who joined in dramatizing the Gospels' historical record, and attempted to save the Son of God from the Jewish "rejection." Jews as "killers of faith" in his Divinity, metamorphosed into actual, bloodthirsty ghouls plotting and clamoring for Jesus' crucifixion. The Gospels' portrayal of Jews conspiring to kill Jesus and participating in his state-sanctioned murder, proves to have been defamation with a theological purpose: to save "Jesus as the Christ" from the influence Jewish rejection of Jesus' Divinity might have on prospective proselytes. Evidence suggests Jews as "killers of faith" in Jesus as the Christ, metamorphosed into Gospel ghouls plotting and clamoring for his crucifixion. The textual gore was a literary tactic intended to threaten prospective proselytes with the hovering talons of the Jewish satan, waiting to carry them off.

B. Why did Simon/Peter turn on the Jews

Simon/Peter would do anything, and did, to silence the Jews who spoke out saying Jesus was not the Christ, but only a rabbi, teacher and healer. His supervised textual atrocities, earlier enumerated (the conspiracy image for equating himself with God; envy over his powers and rejection) culminated in a portrait of "satanic envy," the "Bar-Abbas" libel, elaborated just below.

Prior to summation, the DEFENSE now brings as evidence of the malicious libel permeating the fabric of Gospel canon, in order to expose the historic false accusation the Jews had any least inclination to see harm come to Jesus of Nazareth, whether he believed himself imbued by God's spirit to teach Torah or not; whether he was endowed with a relationship to our Creator enabling him to heal and do wonders, or not:

An analysis of the famed "Barabbas" passage found in the section of each Gospel detailing Pontius Pilate's final judgment of Jesus

In the "Barabbas" episode Jews decide whether Jesus shall live or die and are given that choice by Pontius Pilate. Instead of saving his life, they rabidly insist he be crucified. The DEFENSE asserts the entire Gospel recitation of conjured textual elements are pseudo-canonical accretions, a calumny of false accusations with a central tenet, that the Jews rejected Jesus as the chosen King of the Jews because they were satanic by nature.

The text of Mark 15:12-15:15 introduces the episode:

> "Then (Pilate asked) what shall I do with the man whom you call /is called King of the Jews? And they cried out, 'Crucify him!' And Pilate said to them, 'Why? What evil has he done?' But they shouted more loudly, 'Crucify him!' So Pilate, wishing to satisfy the crowd, released for them Barabbas...and delivered Jesus to be crucified."

[Note: Surmising that Matthias was witness to the mockery of Jesus, we may conclude that he made record of Antipas' guards shouting "crucify him," as attested in John 19:6. The editorial gloss turning Antipas' cohort into heartless Jews constitutes a fragmentation of Matthias' record.]

Intending to demean Jewish elders and priests, the Gospels all join in the invention of Barabbas, a murderer (Mark 15:6), whose release they request instead of Jesus, fulfilling the emperor's (elsewhere, unattested) customary pardon of a criminal in honor of Passover.

Inherent in his criminal nature, Barabbas is more than just a rebel against Rome (as he is depicted in Mark 15:6 to contrast him with Jesus' followers), he is covenanted with a different power—the devil, not God. This idea is expressed in the fantasy name "Bar-Abbas," meaning "son of the father," but which does not exist elsewhere. The Jews prefer freedom for "one of their own," a son of the devil, rather than the Son of God. Put simply, Satan's Progeny they would save—over the Son of God, whose death they ensured.

As tormented and twisted as Jesus on the cross, Christian scripture was dooming Jesus to die by the will of the devil's sons (those who worshipped "Bar-abbas," the Son of Satan, metaphorically, the Jews).

On a technical note, this story neither exhibits the literary form of a midrash nor, strictly speaking, of a parable. Unlike made-up legends that teach a spiritual lesson (the essence of a parable), the Barabbas fiction has no message, lofty or otherwise, about faith or being righteous. It is nothing less than a malevolent slander.

In a last attempt to get the bloodthirsty Jews to change their minds, Pilate offers to free Jesus in honor of Passover. The chief priests and elders stir the crowd to choose the freedom of Barabbas, insisting on Jesus' death sentence, demanding, "Crucify him! Crucify him!"

Literary analysis yields an important result: There is stylistic homogeneity between the Gospel text describing the crowds of Jews attending the so-called judgment of Pilate, from the time Jesus is brought to him until he is taken away to be crucified.

Based on textual deconstruction, the fabricated, vicious Jews supposedly present at the judgment by Pilate, are an authored fabrication stylistically recognizable as originating from the same Gospel editor who created the altogether, transparently vindictive piece of fiction, the saving of Barabbas. In other words, when the "ruthless Jews," high priests, elders and others shout "Crucify him!" the satanic Jews (Barabbas, meaning their "father" was satan) wanted the Christ (the "Son" whose "Father" was God) to die. That was and remains the Gospel message.

From this analysis, the DEFENSE has recovered a germinal source of contempt poisoning the attitudes of early followers of Jesus towards Jews. The "Barabbas" edifice of disfigured belief has as its cornerstone a non-existent Jewish participation in the events leading to the crucifixion. Simon/Peter's textually-supervised diversion of suspicion from Herod Antipas, as elucidated in this **Responsio Iudaeorum**, concealed a desperate effort to save his Christ.

Lest Matthias' unaltered text be canonized, his preserved testimony was fragmented and his name expunged, entombing Jesus' demand that Simon/Peter not make him a god beneath enhanced, poetic language. By confining his rebuke with textual accretions of myriad styles, Simon/Peter's apostolic colleagues in the fledgling Jerusalem church intended to assure the mere-mortal Jesus might never see the light of day, that the one Simon/Peter created might be resurrected to save the faithful.

WHEREFORE:

Quite transparently, the literary embellishment of a crowd of fabricated ghouls screaming "Crucify him," was a canonized defamation that Jews were sons of satan, devotees of "Bar-Abbas."

The DEFENSE concludes this inquiry into the profoundly disquieted frame-of-mind which led at least some of the earliest Disciples, under Simon/Peter's guidance, to portray the Jews as plotting Jesus' death. We have herein set forth the full documentation before you, a Court of Conscience, the necessary facts to convict Herod Antipas, Tetrarch of the Galilee, of orchestrating and bringing to fruition the arrest, hearing, judgment and crucifixion of Jesus.

The primary purpose of this treatise has been to examine the Gospel record contradicting fabricated Jewish antipathy and malevolent plotting to kill Jesus, elements from rejoined textual fragments, which have been miraculously preserved from what increasingly appears to be Matthias' testimony, despite his name having been expunged as the twelfth Disciple following the crucifixion.

This is the Concluding Opinion of the DEFENSE

To say that Jesus was murdered with Jewish complicity not only belies the truth, it is a defamation of immeasurable historic consequence.

Jesus was killed because he had echoed his beloved cousin John the Baptist's public scorn of the tetrarch for committing adultery by taking an illegitimate wife, Herodias, still married according to the Torah, to his living half-brother Philip.

Because Jesus had criticized the tetrarch for violating Torah law, it would not be a stretch to say he was crucified for being an observant Jew.

When, to his utter dismay, he was anointed King of the Jews at the eulogy for John, and confronted Simon/Peter to find out whether he was the one who started that incriminating rumor which had targeted him for sedition, he could only exclaim, "Saying such things about me will get me killed!"

But when Simon/Peter answered "This can never happen to you!" Jesus realized, it seems for the first time, that his lead Disciple saw him as a god, not a man. (In this treatise, Matthew 16:23 and Mark 8:33 are returned to their syntactical originals: "You are walking at the side of a man, not of a god," from the canonized: "You are setting your mind on Divine things not on human things," which is anachronic to the preceding: "Get behind me, Satan" addressed by Jesus to Simon/Peter as they were walking, immediately after the confession that he thought Jesus was King of the Jews.)

Jesus even continued rebuking Simon/Peter with his admonition that he would deny knowing him if he persisted in exalting him as a Divinity.

Jesus had understood that Simon/Peter did not accept the fact he was a mortal; a man, not a god, not a messiah, and not King of the Jews. Therefore, Jesus told Simon/Peter that when he would be arrested, he would deny knowing him; not so much because he was a coward, but because, in Simon/Peter's mind, it was impossible for Jesus, the Son of God, to be vulnerable to mistreatment like an ordinary human being.

In closing

This is the central thesis of the **Responsio Iudaeorum Nostrae Aetatis**:

The Galilean community of observant Jews may have regarded Jesus with a "raised eyebrow," for teaching Torah and synagogue tradition to a group of ignorant locals, perhaps of uncertain Hebrew lineage, and criticized him for over-stepping the limits of rabbinic rules, by healing on Shabbat, or promising his Disciples a place in God's Kingdom, but, they hardly regarded him as claiming to be, or manifesting attributes of Divinity more than any other Jew. To them, whether they should be properly labeled "Pharisees" or "Hasidim/ Pietists," he was a ben-Adam; a human being.

To Simon/Peter, who was exalting him as King of the Jews and the resurrected Son of God, the observant community (Pharisees, Hasidim, rabbinic circles) immutably recalcitrant in their disinterest, was driving a nail of ordinariness into the body of Christ.

Their view of Jesus led him to enjoin on the would-be Jesus-adoring faithful a theology of escape from the satanic talons of the Jews–Jews who were theologically promulgated as intentionally attempting to kill off faith in Jesus, the Christ.

The libelous passages and defamatory content of the Gospels concretized the villainy of the Jew, exposing–and thus avenging– what Simon/Peter perceived as the "attempted killing of faith in Christ."

One may conjecture, without testing the limits of reasonable credibility, that adding to Simon/Peter's contempt was the fact the Jews did not intercede (as if they could) to save their own savior. Paradoxically, the one who, more than any Jew, became the cause of Jesus' fugitive status, as he fled from the seaside eulogy, to Magdala, to Panias, and finally to Jerusalem...having abetted his coronation with proselytizing prior to the eulogy for John, was Simon/Peter. His indoctrinating John's followers, as detailed earlier, even provided Antipas' grounds for the charge of sedition over the cross. If the rejection by ancient, contemporaneous Jews of Jesus' Divinity made them into Simon/Peter's version of spiritual Christ-killers, it did so no more than Jesus himself. Jesus, as put forth in this treatise, was trying to stop Simon/Peter from turning him into a Christ, who he warned he never was, and never believed himself to be.

A Closing Message to the Vatican and All Christians of Good Will

We Jews assert our religious beliefs, whether compatible or contrary to the central messianic tenets of Christianity, are not within the scope of theological concern nor future ajudication in a prophesied era of God's intercession on earth. For there to be a genuine ecumenical revolution, we Jews must no longer be the subject of Christendom's spiritual evaluation, nor subject to a canonized vision of Jesus granting forgiveness, in his anticipated Parousia, weighing our worth as human beings.

With love in our hearts, not contempt or envy, not any sense whatsoever that he equated himself with God, and far more as an embrace of whom we believe he was–a model of compassion for all of us to emulate–we may, today, look back and appreciate Jesus as one of us; a courageous individual who stood up to the overly ritualistic Pietists exclusively separating themselves from less-well Torah educated Jews in the surrounding Galilean villages, to teach a path of concern and caring for the sick and disenfranchised among all people.

Acting god-like did not make him God's Son, but his teachings, often drawn from Torah, as well as his example of compassion, did show us all how to be children of God. With that perception of his ministry in common, we Jews, and all Christians of good conscience,

77

can build a bond strong enough to test any difference which may otherwise pull us asunder.

B'Ezrat Adoshem! With the help of our Creator.

For further information concerning the content of the **Responsio Iudaeorum Nostrae Aetatis** including the critical method of interpretation used to recover the Matthias' text and voice fragmented beneath the canonized Gospels, please feel free to contact Abram Epstein at his Email address: HistoricalTorah@Aol.com

Special acknowledgment and appreciation is given the following two publishers and their editors, for supplementing the author's own translations from the Greek, used in rendering occasional English passages quoted from the Gospels.

Thomas Nelson Publishers, Atlanta.
Gospel Parallels, 1992. Ed. Burton H. Throckmorton
and, Tyndale House Publishers, Carol Stream, Ill.
The New Greek-English Interlinear New Testament, 1990. Ed. J.D. Douglas.

Works Consulted:

1. Gospel Parallels, 1992. Ed. Burton H. Throckmorton. Thomas Nelson Pub. Atlanta.
2. The New Greek-English Interlinear New Testament, 1990. Ed. J.D. Douglas. Pub. Carol Stream, Ill. Tyndale House.
3. Research Study:
Sim, David C., Research Associate: Department of New Testament Studies, Australian Catholic University. Orig. Pub. Cambridge, 2003: "How many Jews became Christians in the first century? The failure of the Christian mission to the Jews"

ABOUT THE AUTHOR

Join a conversation with the author on his
Facebook page: Abram Epstein,
or via Email: HistoricalTorah@Aol.com
or, reach out to him on his Amazon Author's Page

Printed in the United States
By Bookmasters